ARMED AND DANGEROUS

A WRITER'S GUIDE TO WEAPONS

BY MICHAEL NEWTON

Writer's
Digest
Books

CINCINNATI, OHIO

Thanks to Jim Hamby for his careful reading of the manuscript and invaluable advice and comments; and to Sturm, Ruger & Company, Inc., of Southport, Connecticut, and Hammond, Incorporated, of Maplewood, New Jersey, for permissions to reprint the illustrations that appear at the back of the book.

94 93 92 91 90   5 4 3 2 1

Library of Congress Cataloging-in-Publication Data

Newton, Michael
    Armed and dangerous : a writer's guide to weapons / by Michael Newton.
        p.   cm.
    Includes bibliographical references.
    ISBN 0-89879-370-X
    1. Firearms — United States — History. 2. Firearms — History. 3. Explosives, Military — History. 4. Firearms in literature. 5. Explosives, Military, in literature. 6. Adventure stories — Authorship. I. Title.
TS533.2.N49   1990 —   90-12070
683.4'00973 — dc20   CIP

Design by Barbara Seitz

You will acquire a deep understanding of that ancient Christian moral principle, as applied to aimed fire, "It is better to give than to receive."

George Prosser, *Black Politics*, 1968

There's nothing wrong with shooting, as long as the right people get shot.

"Dirty Harry" Callahan

Contents

FATAL ATTRACTION

Guns made this country what it is today.

Too strong, perhaps? Let's check our history.

From colonial times to the space age, firearms have been an integral part of American culture. Our nation's very independence was a matter for debate until some nervous, nameless farmer stood on Concord bridge and fired a shot heard 'round the world. "Old Betsy," Davy Crockett's rifle, was as famous as her owner in the battle for the Alamo. Guns tamed the wild frontier (or stole it from the Mexicans and Indians, depending on your point of view), and in another generation, automatic weapons made the Twenties roar. When the crew of Apollo 11 touched down on the moon, they were armed — just in case.

Despite our protestations to the contrary, Americans have been historically combative, fighting nine great wars and countless smaller conflicts in the past 213 years (including an invasion of the Soviet Union, at Archangel, in 1920). Twenty-three of forty U.S.

presidents had military records, all but one of them in wartime; four saw combat in successive wars, and three were wounded by the enemy.

It may not be precisely true, as Mao Tse-tung suggested, that political power grows from the barrel of a gun, but firearms have frequently altered the course of American government. President Lincoln's assassination in 1865 doomed any hopes of a Civil War cease-fire "with malice toward none," leaving radical Republicans in firm control of reconstruction. (Ten years later, other weapons in the hands of Ku Klux Klansmen and the White Leagues would restore a Democratic "solid South.") The murder of President Mc-Kinley placed Teddy Roosevelt in the White House, thereby inaugurating the progressive era, and gunshots in Dallas slammed the door on Camelot in 1963, obliterating plans for early withdrawal from Vietnam. In 1968 and 1972, presidential front-runners were gunned down in their prime, dramatically revising campaign strategies, and leaving millions of Americans without a candidate to call their own.

As guns have made their mark on history, for good or ill, so they have crept into our common speech. Familiar idioms remind us we should keep our powder dry and caution us against the risk of going off half-cocked. Honest persons are square shooters, while their reckless counterparts are loose cannons, tending to shoot from the hip. If bad news must be tendered, we prefer to take it point-blank, right between the eyes.

Our love affair with lethal hardware carries over into entertainment. Feature films are dedicated to historic firearms (*Winchester '73*), their inventors (*Carbine Williams*), and the individuals who used them in pursuit of gold or glory. Action heroes are defined by their selection of specific weapons, to the point that retail markets are affected. In the early 1970s, the popularity of *Dirty Harry* tripled prices on the Smith and Wesson .44 Magnum revolver; ten years later, terrorists and cocaine cowboys learned about the Ingram submachine gun from *McQ* and other movies, taking on the little "room broom" as their own.

Regardless of your personal opinions on the subject, be they hard line NRA or something more akin to actress Sally Struthers ("traumatized" by the requirement that she fire a pistol in the course of a performance), any writer who observes the marketplace must recognize that firearms play a major role in modern fiction. Cover art is only half the story here. Unless you're writing pure romance, science fiction, or epic fantasy, odds are that *someone* in your story will be packing heat. And if you're doing genre work — historical or Western novels, mysteries, police procedurals, war stories or action/adventure — you will simply have to make your peace with guns. Case closed.

Considering the role that firearms play in modern fiction, it is scandalous to view their handling by authors — major names included — who adopt facades of expertise. I'm not discussing philosophical attitudes toward gun control, but rather technical mistakes and flagrant nonsense which reveal an author's ignorance for all to see. A few exmaples:

• In *The Family*, a novel of the Mafia, author Leslie Waller arms a platoon of security guards with .44 Magnum revolvers, each holding seven rounds in its cylinder, capable of "disemboweling a man at 200 yards." In fact, the .44 — and every other large revolver — holds a maximum of *six* rounds; only .22s and automatics offer the increased capacity.

• In Robert R. McCammon's *Stinger* (and a host of other novels published through the years), assorted heroes check, recheck, and double-check the safety mechanisms on their .38 revolvers — safeties that *do not exist* on any revolver manufactured in this century.

• Adventure writer Mark K. Roberts, in *Jakarta Coup*, describes a Soviet AK-47 assault rifle spitting out 5.56mm bullets, when, in point of fact, the weapon uses 7.62mm ammunition.

• Another veteran action writer, Adam Lassiter, interrupts his novel *Triangle* with a description of the dual "firing handles" on an M-60 machine gun. Anyone who's ever seen the weapon knows the 60 only has *one* "handle"; Lassiter's description properly applies to Maxim-style machine guns from the First World War and certain heavy pieces manufactured later.

• Douglas Fairbairn, in his novel *Shoot*, describes a principal character's private gun collection, including Uzi submachine guns, which have been converted to chamber the 7.62mm NATO round. It sounds impressive, but the plain fact is that submachine guns are designed to handle pistol ammunition; larger rifle cartridges won't fit inside the magazines, no matter how you modify the chamber.

● In *The Evil That Men Do*, Lance Hill presents a fine, authentic-sounding portrait of a magnum-caliber revolver with a silencer attached. Unfortunately (for the author's credibility) it is impossible to "silence" a revolver; Hill is literally blowing smoke.

● Stephen King, in *Cycle of the Werewolf*, drops his furry fiend with silver bullets from a nonexistent ".45 Magnum," proving once and for all that he knows more about werewolves than firearms.

● King also plays fast and loose with his hardware in *The Dark Tower II: The Drawing of the Three*. In the space of five pages, he grafts double triggers onto a Remington slide-action shotgun, introduces a nonexistent "Llama .38 automatic," and discourses at length on the uncontrollable recoil of the M-16 rifle—a weapon specifically designed for minimal kick.

● At the other end of the scale, a manuscript submitted to (and rejected by) Gold Eagle Books described a hero trying to wound himself in the side, for appearance's sake, with a .44 Magnum. Concerned that the bullet may pass through his body and sink the boat in which he's hiding, our macho man solves the problem by placing a pillow behind his back!

Enough, already. There are several explanations for the prevalence of nonsense in descriptive passages involving weapons and firearms identification. One is simple ignorance, which translates into lack of homework. Authors who have problems with their spelling commonly resort to dictionaries (or the spelling programs sold for their computers) to avoid embarrassment. Professionals concerned about the accuracy of their work should find it no more difficult to check out firearms facts—or any other subject—prior to putting words on paper.

Fiction writers, incidentally, are not the only ones who put their ignorance of firearms on display. In his biography of "Baby Face" Nelson (Monarch, 1962), Steve Thurman describes the 1930s outlaw as an expert with the .357 Magnum—a weapon invented the year *after* Nelson's death. And in *The Bad Ones* (Fawcett, 1968), Lew Louderback describes another desperado's final moments thus: "Ma Barker's weapon, a Lewis .300 gas-operated automatic rifle, lay across her body. It was still hot. Forty of its ninety-four rounds were gone." Without belaboring the point, we ought to note that: (a) the Lewis gun was a .303-caliber machine gun, not an automatic rifle; (b) its standard magazines held 47 and 97 rounds, respectively; and (c) an FBI photograph, printed on the page facing Louderback's description, reveals no such weapon in Ma's captured arsenal.

Occasionally, firearms errors are deliberately concocted in an author's bid to "sound dramatic." Thus, we find ourselves confronted with a handgun that—supposedly—will "blow your head *clean* off," a nifty trick with any caliber, considering the human neck's diameter. And, in the same rejected manuscript described earlier, we find the Weatherby Mark V—a bolt action "elephant gun" with a four-round capacity—firing fully automatic from its "big drum magazine."

The most insulting source of technical mistakes in any manuscript arises from the author's own attitude that "it doesn't matter." Arrogant and lazy, certain writers have convinced themselves that no one notices their errors, oversights, and harebrained fabrications. If they slip one past the editor, referring to a nonexistent weapon, it simply proves they're "clever."

And, in fact, they often get away with it. Some editors are sharp enough to check a one-way street's direction on the map or challenge the appearance of a car that wasn't manufactured in a given year. Alas, too many still believe that there are safeties on revolvers and the moon is made of cheese.

Who cares?

The readers.

In the course of writing forty-odd adventure novels and a dozen Westerns, I've discovered that thousands of fans pay attention to "nit-picking" errors on weapons and vehicles, character histories, even geography. No other foul-up produces the flak I receive on mishandling of firearms, from typos misquoting a caliber to more flagrant mistakes in appearance, performance, or whatever else.

As it happens, many action fans are military veterans or currently in service; a significant proportion of the rest hold jobs in law enforcement and related fields. In short, they know their guns, and if an author thinks that he (or she) can slip one past this crowd, he's wrong. Dead wrong.

A fiction writer's first responsibility is turning out a story that will meet his readers' need for action, romance, mystery, suspense. Part of that responsibility (excluding fantasy) involves the deft incorporation of reality — or its illusion — into a story. If the reader is incessantly distracted by mistakes and inconsistencies, he won't enjoy himself, and, incidentally, he may decide to spend his money on another writer, next time out.

This volume is intended as a manual for fiction writers who may not be "gun buffs," but who care enough about their readers and their craft to strive for accuracy. Chapters 2 through 6 are chronologically arranged, providing basic information on the history of firearms from inception to the war in Vietnam. Remaining chapters are divided topically, to cover weapons and firearms identification information useful in the field of modern genre fiction, with a final chapter on explosives. The appendices include a brief chronology of arms development, with tables of firearms identification data relevant to modern handguns and rifles.

Shooting may not be your favorite pastime, and you certainly don't need experience in combat to produce a winning novel, but success in writing — as in any other field — demands some effort. We begin, predictably, at the beginning. . . .

T W O
TOOLS OF ILL OMEN

In the beginning, there were sticks and stones. As early man's capacity for reason grew, he recognized the need for tools—and weapons. There were animals to kill—for meat or skins, in self-defense—and other men were sometimes on the menu. The development of tribes inevitably led to warfare over hunting grounds, the choicest caves, or fishing streams. Invention of the wheel anticipated the development of tanks and armored cars.

I've heard it said, in denigration of the genre, that historical romances are created with one hand on the musket (or the sword) and one hand on the trouser fly. I won't attack the sex-and-violence controversy here, but I suggest that authors of historical romance (or history *without* the romance) ought to know their subject matter. Davy Crockett, for example, never had a zipper in his buckskin trousers, and he never "kilt a bar" with a repeating rifle, either.

What's the point?

Historical fiction, like most other kinds, takes *research*.

I'm not saying that your novel ought to read like some old, dusty text from European Studies 101, but you should bear in mind that readers drawn to history—or fiction based on history—are likely to possess some background knowledge going in. An author in the genre is presumed to have some expertise, and you can blow it in a hurry if you aren't familiar with at least a general chronology of technical and scientific breakthroughs. Weapons lifted out of time and place can damage author credibility with readers, leading to embarrassment and worse.

Beginnings

For openers, a firearm is defined as any tube that uses an explosive charge to hurl projectiles. Air guns, crossbows, slingshots, and assorted other weapons utilizing a mechanical delivery system, minus the explosion, do not qualify. In short, the "fire" is mandatory, and we owe that fire to ancient China.

An early pacifist, Li Ch'uan, was speaking out for generations yet unborn when he denounced the eighth-century arms race, branding weapons in general as "tools of ill omen." His warning fell on deaf ears under the T'ang and Sung dynasties, with Chinese use of gunpowder documented as early as A.D. 1000. Europeans were slow to catch on, with the first reliable reports of a stone-throwing cannon recorded in A.D. 1247 at the battle of Seville. By the second decade of the fourteenth century, no self-respecting European warlord felt his arsenal complete without artillery.

These early weapons were described as *cannon locks*, the first and simplest form of fireams. Loaded through the muzzle, cannon locks consisted of simple tubes, and the various projectiles were packed on top of the explosive powder charge. The cannon lock was fired by application of a flame or burning coal against a touchhole at the rear end of the barrel, thereby setting off the charge.

Velocity and range were obvious advantages of firearms over weapons like the spear or long bow, costing armored knights their previous invincibility. Projectiles might consist of anything from cast iron cannon balls to simple stones, and there are documented incidents of muzzle-loading weapons firing nails and chains, odd bits of scrap iron, even beads of glass. In time, perfection of a hollow cannon ball permitted the insertion of explosive charges or a wad of burning pitch, launching the first incendiary shell.

Predictably, the cannon locks had disadvantages, as well. Gunpowder was *real* powder in those days, before granulation, and considerable wadding — usually soft wood — was needed in between the powder charge and the projectile to provide the necessary pressure. Even so, imperfect seals allowed gas leaks around the wadding, thereby limiting the power and the range of early weapons.

Accuracy was another problem with the cannon locks, and various experiments with hand-held guns were doomed to failure, since the shooter always needed one hand free for application of the lighted coal. This left the weapon's buttstock braced against a shooter's chest or hip, and aiming was impossible. Accordingly, while mounted cannons came to play a vital role in warfare, soldiers of the infantry would fight with bows and lances for the next 160 years.

The Matchlock Era

Our first authenticated record of the revolutionary *matchlock* firearm was reported from Vienna in 1411. As originally conceived, the matchlock had a C-shaped piece of metal pivoted to one side of the weapon's stock, with one end split to hold a "slow match," that is, a piece of hemp fiber treated with saltpeter and other chemicals, designed to burn at a rate of three to five inches per hour. Rotation of the clamp and match made contact with the touchhole, and the weapon — otherwise a normal cannon lock — was fired.

The matchlock, more convenient than its predecessors, with the "fire" attached directly to the gun, soon opened floodgates of invention. *Rifling* — development of straight or spiral lands and grooves inside a weapon's barrel, making bullets spin to stabilize their flight — became the subject of experiments in Italy (and elsewhere) after 1476, increasing both the accuracy and velocity of fired projectiles. *Sights* were also practical, since gunners now had both hands free to aim; by 1500, German marksmen were recording bull's-eyes at 200 yards.

Sporadic efforts to invent repeating matchlocks met with no success, and the results were frequently disastrous. Some matchlocks resembled primitive revolvers, prone to misfire, and development of this particular idea would wait for Samuel Colt, in 1835. Another system called for several charges and projectiles to be tandem-loaded, served by separate touchholes, but faulty ignition produced lethal backfires or fired all the charges at once. Either way, "repeating" matchlocks proved more dangerous to shooters than to their intended targets.

Wheel Locks and Flintlocks

Matchlock weapons revolutionized the role of firearms, both in sport and combat, but they still left much to be desired. In spite of various improvements—sights and rifled barrels—they were still dependent on a lighted "match" to fire the powder charge, and shooters were effectively disarmed by any accident that doused the match. Accordingly, the minds of European armorers were turned toward new ignition systems that would not depend upon a burning coal or open flame.

The *wheel lock*, credited to German craftsmen circa 1517, resolved the problem nicely, with a mechanism still employed in cigarette lighters. A pull of the wheel lock's trigger spun a serrated wheel, producing sparks from contact with a stationary flint; the sparks, in turn, ignited priming powder in the weapon's touchhole, flashing through to fire the loaded charge. No open flame was necessary, and in stormy weather, priming charges—unlike soggy matches—could easily be replaced.

Invention of the wheel lock led to other new developments. Because the trigger pull was relatively heavy, using force to spin the wheel and thereby jeopardizing accuracy, new *set triggers* were developed on a basic principle still used in modern guns. By pushing one arm of the trigger while the piece was cocked, a wheel lock was preset so that a touch upon the second trigger fired the gun without shifting off target. Likewise, a bewildering variety of *safeties*, both mechanical and manual, were added to prevent the touchy wheel locks from discharging accidentally.

The *snaphaunce*, introduced in 1525, supplanted the expensive wheel lock with a simple adaptation of the matchlock firing mechanism. In place of the outmoded "match," the weapon's hammer held a piece of pyrites, with a steel point—dubbed the "anvil"—mounted near the touchhole. Impact of the flint on steel produced a shower of sparks above the priming charge and thereby fired the weapon. Inexpensive and reliable, the snaphaunce marked another stage of firearms evolution, serving as the inspiration for another generation of inventors.

Flintlock weapons, traceable to French inventors in the early seventeenth century, improved on the snaphaunce design by adding a hinged steel cover for the priming pan. The falling hammer struck the hinged piece (called a "batterie" or "frizzen"), and the impact threw it open to reveal the priming powder; sparks were generated by the flint and steel, the priming powder flashed through a touchhole, and the weapon fired. Protection of the priming charge from wind and rain permitted riflemen to function in conditions where their weapons had been previously rendered useless, thus promoting firearms as a more effective weapon on the battlefield.

In 1690, British military leaders formally adopted flintlock muskets for their troops. The arms were commonly referred to as "Brown Bess," in reference to the color of their barrels and the myth that they had been adopted under Queen Elizabeth I — deceased for eighty-seven years before the muskets were procured! French troops officially adopted flintlocks in 1746, while Prussia curiously lagged behind, finally upgrading its arsenal in 1808.

Invention of the flintlock marked a watershed in firearms evolution, as it was the final alteration based entirely on mechanical revision of the firing system. Chemistry would play a major role in future stages of development, as armorers dispensed with flint and steel.

America in Arms

Despite their omnipresence in the colonies, firearms receive scant attention in early historical records. We know that many settlers carried matchlock weapons from their native lands, and Massachusetts troops were issued snaphaunce arms in 1628, but little else is clear about the arming of Colonial America. The crudest pieces dazzled aborigines in early clashes with the colonists, but soon those "Indians" were shooting back, while wars between the English, French, and Spanish empires carried lethal repercussions into the New World. Arms were needed, and in quantity, to hold the line.

The first scientific approach to firearms manufacture in America was made by German settlers in Pennsylvania. These craftsmen revolutionized the loading process by wrapping smaller-caliber bullets in linen or buckskin soaked in tallow, thus improving on the European system where bullets were started down the barrel with a mallet, then punched home with a ramrod. At the same time, lubricated wrapping made a better gas check in the weapon's rifled barrel, thereby increasing accuracy and effective range. These early guns have entered history erroneously as "Kentucky rifles," as they were the favorite arms of pioneers exploring land between the Cumberlands and Mississippi River, later dubbed Kentucky.

Our earliest official military arms were smoothbore flintlock muskets, weighing roughly ten pounds each, in calibers ranging from .72 to .80. (*Caliber* refers to the diameter of a selected firearm's barrel, measured out in hundredths of an inch. Thus, a .25-caliber bullet is one quarter-inch in diameter, and so on.) By the outbreak of the Revolution, most official troops were using muskets designated as the 1763 Model, a slight variation on the weapon adopted by France in 1746.

Despite their awesome calibers, smoothbores were notoriously inaccurate and slow in reloading; their primary value in combat consisted of laying down smoke screens to cover a bayonet charge. Attackers were normally able to cover the smoothbore's effective killing range — a hundred-yard maximum — before defending troops could load and fire a second volley. Most battles in the European theater were still decided by the bayonet and cavalry . . . but times were changing.

Shortages of ready cash and the erratic methods of conscription guaranteed that many rebel soldiers in the Revolution would be forced to arm themselves with guns from home. This meant that British redcoats were confronted by the highly accurate "Kentucky" rifles, in addition to the standard smoothbores. Casualties inflicted on the British troops at Bunker Hill and elsewhere clearly demonstrated the effectiveness of rifled arms, compelling officers on both sides to reevaluate their antiquated strategies. While colonists resorted to guerrilla warfare in the forests, their opponents grudgingly began to lay Brown Bess aside, experimenting cautiously with rifles.

Major Patrick Ferguson was Britain's shining star of weapons research. An extraordinary marksman and inventor of the first breech-loading flintlock rifle used in England, Ferguson had been specifically assigned to kill George Washington at Germantown, by sniping him across the smoky battlefield. The major found his target, but could not believe a general officer would dress so casually, and so concluded Washington was not on hand. Ferguson later led the Tory forces trapped by rebels at King's Mountain, and he died there on October 7, 1780, in a battle that proved the superiority of American marksmen. Ferguson's troops surrendered after a sniper cut him down; by that time, 400 out of 1,100 Tory soldiers had been killed or wounded.

Pistols, through the early nineteenth century, were basically the same as long guns in their firing mechanisms. Smoothbore flintlocks for the most part, they were usually carried by officers and members of the cavalry, the latter having little use for rifles as they needed one hand free to rein their mounts. Americans had no "official" pistol prior to 1806, and handguns used throughout the Revolution came in varied shapes and sizes. General Washington preferred a pair of .67-caliber pistols, manufactured in London by Hawkins and Wilson around 1749.

Artillery was vital to the revolutionary effort, but designs did not keep pace with changing trends in firearms. Field pieces still employed the cannon lock design, and *mortars* — stubby cannons fired with muzzles elevated to project their shells beyond obstructions such as walls — were used to good effect at Fort Ticonderoga and elsewhere. Cannons, through the latter nineteenth century, were typically described in terms of *pounds*, referring to the weight of their projectiles. Thus, a twelve-pounder fired cannon balls weighing twelve pounds each. Mortars, on the other hand, were normally described in *inches*, based on muzzle diameter.

Percussion Arms

The next great stride in firearms evolution, development of the *percussion lock*, was made by Rev. Alexander Forsythe, a Scotsman, in 1793. Forsythe's guns used fulminate of mercury — a chemical explosive sensitive to impact — as a substitute for priming powder. Detonated by a falling hammer, the explosive "pills" produced ignition in the firing chamber and eliminated problems for the marksmen who had found it difficult to keep their powder dry.

In the United States, large numbers of "Kentucky" flintlock rifles were converted into *pill locks*, their priming pans replaced with small iron bowls, and hammers fitted with projections to explode the "pill." Kentucky rifles thus became "Plains rifles," used to tame the wild frontier throughout the first half of the nineteenth century. Plains rifles generally weighed between 6.5 and 10.5 pounds, chambered in calibers ranging from .26 to .40. Still muzzle loaders, their barrels ranged in length from 26 to 38 inches, occasionally longer. These were, in short, the standard weapons of the mountain men, the long hunters and Indian fighters, carried far and wide on the westward march of Manifest Destiny.

The introduction of percussion arms, while revolutionary in its impact, did not wipe out flintlocks overnight. The first official military pistol in America — and all of it successors through the early 1830s — would be flintlocks, demonstrating the classic military resistance to change. American troops in the War of 1812 were basically armed with rifles from the Revolutionary period, but they retained their legendary skills in marksmanship. In the anticlimactic battle of New Orleans, Wellington's redcoats advanced through withering fire to assault hidden riflemen, suffering 2,000 casualties against eight Americans dead and thirteen wounded. The horrendous massacre should have logically rendered shock tactics obsolete, but commanders stubbornly refused to learn, and their intransigence would be repaid in blood at Gettysburg.

Officers and cavalrymen in the "second war for independence" carried flintlock pistols dubbed the "Harper's Ferry model 1806." Remaining in service through 1819, the side arms would be replaced by a series of flintlock successors through the early 1840s, when conversion to percussion arms began. The U.S. Model 1842 percussion pistol was a modified edition of the flintlock issued during 1836, equipped to use the Maynard *tape primer*, a "cap-roll" design preserved for posterity through its use in children's cap guns.

Likewise, military buyers shifted to percussion rifles with the Model 1841, a weapon variously dubbed the "Mississippi," the "Harper's Ferry rifle," or the "Yaeger" — a corruption of the German "Jaeger." Carried by American troops in the war with Mexico, the Model 1841 accounted for the slaughter of Mexican cavalry at Buena Vista in February 1847, dropping five of the enemy for every American killed or wounded.

Breechloaders

Through the early 1840s, all successful firearms had been muzzle-loaders, with the built-in limitation of clumsy reloading, but inventors were persistent in their efforts to develop more efficient weapons loaded through the breech (the rear end of the barrel, closest to the shooter). Christian Sharps broke ground in 1848, by patenting the *drop block* action, easily the most important breakthrough of its time. So revolutionary was the concept that it still saw use in more than forty types of rifles at the start of World War II.

The Sharps design was operated by lowering a hinged trigger-guard lever, dropping the breechblock to permit insertion of a paper cartridge. Reversing the trigger-guard action automatically closed the breech, shearing off one end of the cartridge to facilitate ignition. Later versions of the rifle were modified to accept metallic cartridges, and some were sturdy enough to operate as muzzle-loaders if the breeches fouled! Ideal for hunting buffalo and fighting Indians alike, the Sharps would leave its mark on history as settlers continued pushing westward to the sea.

While no competitor approached the ultimate success of Christian Sharps, a few produced significant breech-loading weapons. The Burnside — named for its inventor, Union General A.F. Burnside — used a special brass cartridge of conical design, with a hole at the rear to let percussion caps flash through and detonate the charge. The Gallagher was operated by a trigger-guard lever that swung the barrel forward and down, to facilitate loading of a paper cartridge. The Maynard used a freak brass cartridge, with the barrel hinged for rapid loading. Gilbert Smith's carbine (i.e., a short rifle) was also hinged at the breech, like today's common shotgun, chambering a cartridge molded from India rubber.

With perfection of the breech-loading system, firearms moved into a transitional stage, marked by experimentation with self-contained cartridges, marrying bullets with premeasured ignition charges. These developments, in turn, facilitated new experiments with rapid-fire repeaters, which were totally impractical with muzzle-loading arms.

The first significant repeating rifle was the Jennings, patented in 1849. A magazine atop the breech was loaded with percussion pills, while bullets with propellant charges packed inside their hollow bases filled a tube below the barrel. The shooter's index finger passed through a ring forming the end of a lever below the receiver; his thumb was on the hammer, and with the weapon's muzzle elevated slightly, gravity delivered a bullet to the carrier. As the hammer was drawn and the lever pushed forward, the breech pin moved back and the carrier rose, placing the cartridge in line with the barrel. Pulling the lever back forced the breech pin forward, driving the cartridge into the firing chamber; the same motion dropped a primer from the magazine by action of a revolving rack. The weapon fired by upward pressure of the shooter's index finger in the ring, and there were no spent casings to eject. With a capacity of 24 rounds, the Jennings was indeed a formidable weapon.

The Volcanic rifle, a direct descendant of the Jennings, was developed during 1854. Its primitive lever action was later improved in the Henry and Winchester rifles, making the Volcanic a true "missing link" in firearms evolution. The spring-loaded magazine contained patented "Volcanic" cartridges (hollow-based bullets containing black powder, the charges sealed with cardboard discs incorporating built-in primers), and the weapon's accuracy is suggested by a modern test, which placed five rounds inside a 21-inch circle at a range of 80 yards. Despite its various advantages — and its performance in police hands during Staten Island rioting in 1858 — the Volcanic rifle had virtually disappeared from circulation by 1860.

Metallic cartridges were yet another breakthrough in the evolution of repeating arms. Modern breech-loading ammunition must meet three criteria: (1) the cartridge must be "fixed," or self-contained, with the projectile, primer, and propellant in a single package; (2) ductile metal casings must expand against the firing chamber walls on detonation, serving as a gas-check to the rear; and (3) the primer must include a built-in mechanism to permit its detonation under impact of the firing pin. These factors make it possible for marksmen to reload and fire their weapons at a speed impossible when cartridges had to be assembed on the spot from three or four components.

The first successful breech-loading cartridge, dubbed the *pinfire*, was introduced in 1836. The cartridge case was made of paper, but a metal head contained the priming mixture in a cup-shaped base. Pinfire weapons had a notch in which the firing pin was settled once a cartridge had been loaded. When the hammer fell, it drove the firing pin against the primer and produced ignition, setting off the main propellant charge.

A more efficient cartridge was the *rimfire*, still in use with modern .22-caliber weapons. The case head has a small projecting rim, with priming spun between the folds, and impact anywhere along that rim will fire the charge. The first practical rimfire cartridge — a .22 developed by Smith and Wesson — was introduced in 1857. Three years later, rimfire cartridges would also feed the famous Henry repeater.

The *centerfire* cartridge, developed in England during 1861, seats its primer in the center of a metal case head, thereby permitting cartridges to be reloaded after use (a thrifty process still impossible with rimfires). Centerfire technology permitted the development of new high-powered cartridges in military and civilian arms. With the exception of .22-caliber weapons and rare experimental pieces, modern arms universally employ centerfire cartridges.

A House Divided

The American Civil War (1861-65) marked a watershed in arms development. Generally acknowledged as the first "modern" conflict, our War Between the States introduced barbed wire and trench warfare, hand grenades and land mines, armored trains and ironclad ships, aerial reconnaissance and submarine vessels, machine guns, and even a primitive flamethrower, described as "a small garden engine" spewing Greek fire.

Still, for all its innovation, the outbreak of civil war found both sides largely unprepared. The Union army had 530,000 muskets in its arsenal, but they were basically modified arms of the Revolutionary era, fitted out with rifled barrels and percussion locks. They were still muzzle-loaders, a design so popular with military minds that 10,000 more would be manufactured in the first year of the war, 200,000 in the second year, 500,000 in the third. The Union also purchased 726,705 European muzzle-loaders to be on the "safe" side, including 428,000 Enfield .577-calibers, manufactured in England.

Despite their popularity with conservative buyers, muzzle-loaders were notoriously — and dangerously — inefficient under stress of combat, when misfires and panic often resulted in misloading and jamming of weapons. Following the carnage at Gettysburg, 37,574 discarded muskets were recovered from the battlefield, nearly half of them jammed due to improper loading. Of the weapons recovered, 12,000 had two rounds in the barrel, 6,000 held from three to ten rounds each, and one was jammed with no less than twenty-three bullets!

A failed attempt to finally replace the muzzle-loaders was initiated with the introduction of the Palmer carbine, patented in December 1863. The first weapon to use a bolt-locking system for metallic cartridges, this .52-caliber rimfire weapon featured a spring extractor on top of the bolt, an automatic ejector, and a cut-away receiver on the side to make ejection positive. (It also had a large thumb-cocking hammer added as an afterthought, at the insistence of military procurers who liked their modern arms to look traditional.) In practice, however, the single-shot breech-loader never caught on, and only 1,001 had been issued by war's end.

In spite of countless problems, Civil War rifles were more lethal than ever before, thanks to introduction of the Minié ball—a conical bullet invented by a Frenchman, introduced in England during 1851. Designed to expand in the grooves of a barrel on firing, the Minié ball increased effective range from 100 to 500 yards, thereby making defense five times more effective, assault over open ground five times more costly. The Minié ball helped initiate trench warfare fifty years before World War I, and it was largely responsible for the Civil War's awesome casualty rate: 24,400 cut down in two days at Shiloh; 34,500 in two days at Chickamauga; more than 50,000 in three days at Gettysburg. After the battle of Malvern Hill, in which 5,500 Confederates fell in a single charge, General D.H. Hill remarked, "It was not war; it was murder."

New repeating rifles also did their part in raising body counts. The Spencer, patented in 1860, was the first successful repeater to use metallic cartridges. A spring-loaded magazine tube in the buttstock held seven rounds, fired by an external hammer, with the action operated by a trigger-guard lever. After a personal audition for President Lincoln in 1861, military tests led to the purchase of 70,000 Spencers by the end of the war, at a total cost of nearly $3 million.

The Henry repeater, a lever action descendant of the Volcanic design, was patented in March of 1860. A tubular magazine below the barrel held twelve .44-caliber rimfire cartridges, and the weapon boasted a rate of fire close to 25 rounds per minute. The action of a trigger-guard lever ejected spent casings, chambered a fresh round, and cocked the hammer simultaneously, thereby eliminating one more wasted movement on the shooter's part. Despite its lethal potential, the Henry design failed to rival the Spencer's acceptance. Only 1,731 rifles were purchased by the Union army, with another 10,000 sold privately for use by individual state regiments. Still, the Henry saw action on Sherman's march through Georgia, and it would survive to leave its mark upon the West in years to come.

Revolving pistols were another military innovation of the Civil War. The first successful six-gun had been patented by American Samuel Colt in England during 1835. He secured a U.S. patent the following year, and his Colt Model 1860, a .44-caliber cap-fired percussion piece, became the principal side arm during the war, with 200,000 revolvers maufactured on order from Washington.

Regardless of their innovation, early Colts—and most other revolvers—were still muzzle-loaders, now boasting five or six chambers in place of one. They were also *single-action* pieces, meaning that the shooter was required to cock the hammer prior to every shot, his action rotating the weapon's cylinder and bringing (hopefully!) a fresh charge under the hammer. Conversely, *double-action* weapons may be fired by simple pressure on the trigger, starting with the hammer down. First pressure on the trigger draws the hammer back and rotates the cylinder simultaneously; when the trigger "breaks" (its second—i.e., *double*—action), the hammer is released to strike the priming cap or firing pin.

While Colts would dominate the field of battle in the Civil War, they were not out there by themselves. The Union army also purchased 125,314 Remington .44 single-action revolvers, along with various lesser-known side arms. The Starr Army model was a double-action piece in .44 caliber, some 48,000 of which were pressed into duty by Union commanders. The Savage Navy revolver, a percussion piece chambered in .36 caliber, sold more than 11,000 units during the war, while the Pettingill Army model, a double-action .44, fared worse, delivering only 2,000 copies of the first (and only) U.S. military hammerless revolver. Lagging far behind, the Joslyn Army revolver, a .44 percussion arm designed to hold five rounds instead of six, contributed 1,100 weapons to the conflict.

A desire to kill large numbers in a hurry led to further innovations in the field of rapid-fire weapons. *Volley guns* were frequently employed by both sides, nicknamed "covered bridge guns" because they were ideally suited to mowing down ranks of men in confined spaces. A typical volley gun (and the best known) was the Requa Battery, an awesome .58-caliber weapon whose twenty-five barrels lay side-by-side on a wheeled cart. The sliding breech mechanism was loaded with individual steel chambers, powder and ball being loaded in the same style as early flintlocks. With the breech locked, a train of powder was laid across twenty-five open touchholes, one percussion cap lighting the train and discharging the barrels in rapid succession.

The first true machine gun was designed by a Confederate captain named Williams during 1861. Essentially a rapid-fire cannon, the weapon fired a one-pound shell from its 1.57-inch bore, the mechanism being operated by a hand crank. Fed with self-consuming paper cartridges, the piece was capable of firing 65 rounds per minute with fair accuracy. A battery of the guns was used effectively against Union troops in the battle at Seven Pines, Virginia, on May 3, 1862.

Another revolutionary model was the famous Gatling gun, patented in 1862. The initial model had six barrels, chambered for .58-caliber rimfire cartridges. Despite the gun's occasional appearance in "historic" films and television programs, Gatlings saw no action in the Civil War. Suspected as a "closet" rebel sympathizer, Dr. Richard Gatling was rejected when he offered his invention to the Union army. (Post-war tests resulted in adoption of a one-inch model by the military, and the guns were also used at Arizona's Yuma prison, to reverse the rising tide of jailbreaks.)

As every high school student knows (or should know), the Confederacy was an agricultural society, dependent on the North for manufactured items such as farm machinery, shoes — and firearms. Cut off from their major source of weapons, separated from the European market by a federal blockade, the rebels were compelled to fall back on initiative and ingenuity. The Williams machine gun provides one example; another was the *R.L. Hunley*, an eight-man submarine vessel launched at Mobile, which torpedoed the U.S.S. *Housatonic* in February 1864 and went down with her prey. Confederate officers also debated the feasibility of chemical warfare, anticipating World War I in their discussion of shells designed to emit "offensive gases" and produce a "suffocating effect."

For all their native ingenuity, the Southern troops were doomed — if not from the beginning, certainly after the bloody killing fields of Gettysburg. Outnumbered and outgunned, the Confederacy was compelled to raise a flag of truce at Appomattox courthouse, but the end of the Civil War would bring no ceasefire to America. Beyond the Mississippi, there were buffaloes to slaughter, Indians to fight, and towns to tame. The west was getting wild, and there was gunsmoke in the wind.

T H R E E
HOW THE WEST WAS REALLY WON

Our nation's history, from Plymouth Rock to the admission of Alaska and Hawaii, is a story of expansion to the west, and yet our "Wild West" period is rather narrowly defined. Historians generally agree upon the years from 1865 to 1890 as the cut-off points, although some films and novels carry Western action through the early 1900s—even, in *The Wild Bunch*, to the eve of World War I. Dramatic license notwithstanding, the established quarter-century incorporates completion of the first transcontinental railroads (and the first train robbery), the Indian wars, the rise and decline of the great cattle empires, the gunfighter era, and the closing of the open range through enactment of federal legislation granting large tracts of land to settlers at little or no cost. The era's casualties included man and animal alike—Native Americans, bison, passenger pigeons, sheep by the thousands, and an uncertain number of self-styled "fast guns."

An author anxious to succeed in Western fiction should remember that a large percentage of his readers are, in essence, amateur historians themselves. The Western novel is not meant to stand as history, but certain basic research is required to rescue authors from embarrassment at introducing telephones, repeating rifles, and the like before these objects were invented. If you plan to have your Western hero packing a machine gun — as does "Captain Gringo" in the *Renegade* adventures — you must lay the proper groundwork in advance. Be warned: Your editors and readers aren't prepared to take bizarre diversions from the Western "formula" on faith alone.

"The Only Good Indian . . ."

The first Thanksgiving aside, American Indians were widely viewed as a dangerous roadblock to westward expansion and the relentless march of Manifest Destiny. The red men have been moving targets for white marksmen since 1609, when Samuel de Champlain killed two Iroquois chiefs and wounded a third with one blast from his trusty arquebus, thus introducing the aborigines to firepower (and simultaneously defeating the first "bullet-proof" vest, fashioned from twigs). Across the next 250 years, Indians and whites massacred one another with fair regularity, but historic discussion of "The Indian Wars" properly concerns itself with action west of the Mississippi, between 1865 and the final bloodbath at Wounded Knee, South Dakota, in December 1890.

Colorado militiamen, under Colonel John Chivington, got a jump on the main action in November 1864, assaulting Chief Black Kettle's camp at Sand Creek under orders to "kill and scalp all Indians." Anticipating the Vietnam era of inflated body counts, Chivington claimed between 400 and 500 Indians slain, but a battlefield tally reduced the number to 163, at least 110 of them unarmed women and children. The militia suffered 47 casualties, with nine men killed — apparently resulting from an overzealous spray of "friendly fire."

Black Kettle managed to survive Sand Creek, but his luck ran out four years later, almost to the day, when George Custer's 7th Cavalry staged another surprise raid at Washita River, in Texas. Of 103 red casualties, only eleven were braves, with Black Kettle among them. In celebration of his victory, Custer also ordered the slaughter of several hundred Indian ponies corralled at the camp.

The moccasin was on the other foot in June 1876, when Custer and 212 of his men were cut off and killed at the battle of Little Big Horn, but the Indians were never victorious for long. Hopelessly outnumbered and outgunned, their last gasp came in 1890, when at least 150 helpless Sioux were killed by troops employing rapid-fire repeating cannons. Once again, most of the 68 whites killed or wounded fell before the guns of their own comrades, caught up in the frenzy of the turkey shoot.

Aside from the experimental use of various repeating rifles, none of which were formally adopted, soldiers on the plains were armed with Springfield carbines, single-shots designed to fire a .50-caliber projectile. The metallic cartridges were loaded and ejected through a trapdoor in the top of the receiver, thus allowing soldiers to achieve a fairly rapid rate of fire, as single-shots go. After 1873, many of the carbines were chambered for the new .45-70 round (denoting a .45-caliber bullet, propelled by 70 grains of black powder).

Red men, on the other hand, were not restricted by the narrow bounds of military thinking, and the plains tribes welcomed new advances in repeating rifles as the guns became available. Proficient shots with Spencers, Henrys, and the new lever-action Winchester repeaters—which they captured from fallen enemies or purchased from white traders in violation of federal law—Indian warriors took full advantage of new firearms technology in an effort to balance the odds. As they had taken to the horse upon its introduction by the Spaniards, so the red men now became the finest mounted marksmen in the world . . . but it was not enough.

If military minds seemed frozen on the subject of repeating rifles, they were more elastic in regard to other weapons. The revolver had already proved itself in combat, and with the Indian wars well under way, Washington adopted the new Colt Model 1873 as the official military side arm. Chambered in .45 caliber, the Colt '73 was a revision of the 1860 model, with a new ejector rod and loading gate, permitting cartridges to be unloaded and replaced individually, with the hammer on half-cock instead of removing the whole cylinder. The Cavalry model '73 featured a 7.5-inch barrel, while the Infantry and Artillery models sported barrels two inches shorter.

Mr. Gatling's gun, in .50 caliber, had been adopted by the

military during 1865, and it saw rugged duty on the plains. Different models were produced, with six and ten barrels respectively, but the weight of the latter restricted them to service in fixed fortifications, and they were sold primarily to European buyers.

Another weapon, similar in appearance to the Gatling but unique in design, was the Hotchkiss gun, a 1.5-inch rapid-fire cannon introduced around 1881. The weapon featured five barrels, mounted parallel to one another on a central axis, held in place between two metal discs. A hand crank on the right caused the barrels to rotate and fire, while individual rounds were loaded through a chute on the upper left of the receiver. Awesome in their rate of fire, the Hotchkiss guns were used at Wounded Knee to slaughter Indians who ran beyond the range of soldiers' carbines. Detonation of their high-explosive shells was deemed responsible for many casualties on both sides of the "battle" that effectively annihilated Indian resistance on the plains.

Annihilating Species

As red men were considered obstacles to progress, so were certain animals regarded as a nuisance or a threat along the great frontier. It is impossible to calculate how many bison roamed the plains, from Texas north to Canada, before the white man drove his railroads west, but conservative estimates place their number in the neighborhood of 15 million. The majority of those comprised the "southern herd," at large from Kansas to the Rio Grande, while relatively smaller numbers formed a "northern herd" between the Jayhawk State and North Dakota, westward through Wyoming.

Bison were a double problem for the white man, rudely holding up the progress of his railroad crews while simultaneously furnishing the Indians with food and clothing, tools and weapons, even fuel for camp fires (in the form of dried dung). Considering the temper of the times, there was but one solution, and it emanated from the barrel of a gun.

It took a decade to annihilate the southern herd, beginning in the spring of 1868, although the final fifty specimens would not be hunted down and slaughtered until 1887. Of the estimated 3.7 million bison killed in two years' time, from 1872 to 1874, roughly 150,000 were killed by plains Indians; the rest were shot and skinned by "sportsmen," left to rot in reeking mountains as the slaughter took on trappings of official military policy. When a delegation of concerned Texans approached Gen. Philip Sheridan to discuss the wisdom of wholesale annihilation, Sheridan replied, "Let them [the hunters] kill, skin, and sell until the buffalo is exterminated, as it is the only way to bring lasting peace and allow civilization to advance." By 1879, civilization was advancing on the northern herd, and the hunters worked themselves out of business in five years, reporting a near-total absence of targets by 1884.

Most of the hapless bison were killed with Sharps single-shot rifles, manufactured in heavy weights and calibers for professional "buffalo" hunters between 1875 and the early 1880s. The Sharps "Big Fifty" was a special favorite, with hunters using telescopes to make their kills at ranges of 1,000 yards. For what it's worth, the term "sharpshooter" is a tribute to the guns and marksmen that combined to clear the plains of game.

Another popular single-shot weapon for large game was the Peabody *falling block* system, patented in July 1862. This weapon had its breechblock hinged at the rear, below the line of the barrel bore, and its action was unlocked by pulling the trigger-guard down and forward, thereby lowering the front end of the block for rapid loading. Originally chambered in .45 rimfire, the Peabody was tested by the Army in 1862, but the Civil War ended before purchasers could make up their collective bureaucratic minds. In later years, competing manufacturers produced a score of variations on the Peabody design.

A third powerful single-shot rifle, the Remington *rolling block*, was patented in January 1863. The mechanism for locking the Remington's breech consisted of two parts. One, the breechblock itself, was a heavy rolling member mounted in the receiver on an axis pin, with the firing pin located in a hole through its center face. The breechblock was fitted with a thumb extension lever, allowing it to be rolled away from the breech when its locking support was withdrawn. A second component, the firing hammer, pivoted on an axis pin behind the breechblock. In the Remington design, the breechblock was spring-supported against the face of the breech when ready to fire, securing the action for heavy calibers required to kill at long range.

While bison are remembered as a leading casualty of conquest, isolated members of the species managed to survive the sixteen years of carnage. Passenger pigeons were less fortunate, their species hounded to extinction with an estimated 1 *billion* birds shot or trapped in 1878 alone. Most of those were killed with shotguns, modern versions of the ancient fowling pieces that we have not heretofore discussed. Initially designed for dropping birds in flight, these smoothbore weapons fired a spray of pellets—known as "shot"—that boosted the shooter's chance of scoring on a moving target. Though created for the sportsman, shotguns also had potential in the antipersonnel department, as we shall observe.

[A brief digression. Note that shotguns are described in terms of "gauge" (or "bore," in Britain), rather than the more familiar "caliber." Historically, a weapon's gauge was calculated on the number of lead balls, equal to the diameter of the gun's barrel, that add up to one pound in weight. Thus, the larger the weapon, the smaller its gauge, with a 12-gauge shotgun larger than a 20-gauge, and so forth. Shot is also named and numbered on the basis of its size, with smaller pellets designated as birdshot, the heavier buckshot reserved for larger game—or human beings. As with shotguns, smaller numbers indicate a larger pellet, so that #1 shot is considerably larger and more lethal than a #9 projectile.]

Shotguns, by their nature and design, have shorter range than rifles, since the shot begins to spread at once and quickly loses its momentum. In the latter 1860s, range and accuracy were improved with introduction of the "choke," a method of constricting shotgun muzzles slightly, in an effort to control the pattern of the shot. A choke's efficiency is measured in terms of "pattern density"—that is, the average number of pellets striking inside a 30-inch circle at a range of 40 yards. The early chokes, ironically, were more efficient than our current models, offering 90 percent pattern density against a modern maximum of 70 percent. With the improvement, hunters found it possible to slaughter birds with more efficiency, at higher altitudes, and so they swept the Great Plains clean of pigeons in a few short months.

Head 'em Up and Move 'em Out

The cowboy era was inaugurated during 1867, with completion of the railhead at Abilene and the first long drives from Texas. By 1872, some 700,000 head of cattle had been shipped eastward from Kansas, with the industry's boom period arriving between 1875 and

1885. Thereafter, a rapid decline was precipitated by fencing of the open range, new laws restricting interstate commerce, and severe weather that decimated herds in the mid-1880s. All told, the stereotypical cowboy was active for barely two decades, but his breed left an indelible mark on American culture.

Guns were primarily tools to the cowboy, less important — and generally less pampered — than his horse and lariat. Colt six-guns were the favored side arms of the period, used variously for killing snakes, dispatching injured livestock, and turning stampedes. At trail's end, they were also useful for "hurrahing the town," a drunken ritual that involved cowboys riding wild through the streets, firing aimlessly into the air (and, occasionally, through storefront windows). When not so employed, the cowboy's six-gun often doubled as a makeshift hammer or a pry-bar, and was seldom carefully maintained.

Repeating rifles found more favor with the cowboys than with big-game hunters or the narrow-minded military, providing rapid and accurate firepower against marauding Indians and bands of rustlers who whittled down the herds on every drive. Numerous Henry repeaters were still in circulation, although the company dissolved in 1866, but new lever-action Winchesters were clearly the wave of the future.

Founded at New Haven, Connecticut, in 1866, the Winchester Repeating Arms Company produced its first rifle that same year, adding a modified magazine to the old Henry design. Chambered in .44-caliber rimfire, the Winchester Model 1866 held sixteen rounds (or fourteen, in the carbine), and was manufactured through 1898, with 170,000 guns sold. Designed as a civilian firearm, it was eagerly adopted for military use by the Turkish defenders at Plevna, who used the Winchester '66 to kill 30,000 Russians in 1877.

Winchester's most popular rifle, hands down, was the Model 1873, with 720,000 guns sold before it was discontinued in 1919. Initially chambered in .44-40, subsequent versions were manufactured to accommodate the .38-40 cartridge (in 1880) and the .32-30 (in 1882). Other Winchesters of the cowboy era included the Model 1876, initially chambered in .45-47 (with 63,871 sold prior to discontinuation in 1897), and the Model 1886, chambered for the .45-70 Government cartridge. All were of excellent quality and design, providing cowboys and settlers alike with state-of-the-art firepower.

With the gradual decline of the open range, cattle barons unleashed their frustration — and their hired gunmen — in a series of range wars aimed at two primary targets. First of those were the homesteaders, derided as "squatters," who took advantage of government land grants to settle and populate the plains. While clashes did occur in several areas, their impact — and their body count — has been (predictably) exaggerated in the realm of fiction. Wyoming's Johnson County war — subject of the long-winded film *Heaven's Gate* — erupted in 1892 after cattlemen compiled a "death list" of 70-odd squatters marked for extermination. In fact, only two of the targets were slain, in a single shooting incident, before the countryside rose en masse and arrested the hit men, holding them for trials which exposed the conspiracy and spelled disaster for the stockmen in Johnson County.

Shepherds and their flocks drew more attention from the cattlemen than squatters in the last days of the cowboy era, with endemic violence lasting through the early 1900s. No more than thirty human casualties have been documented from the various "sheep wars," but sheep were frequently slaughtered en masse. Wyoming raiders killed 12,000 sheep in a single night, in 1904, and Oregon's Crook County Sheep Shooters Association claimed 10,000 kills in their first active season. That same year — again in Wyoming — 4,000 sheep belonging to one shepherd were slaughtered by riders who also killed his dogs and burned his camp. The inoffensive sheep were variously shot or bludgeoned, driven over cliffs and into rivers, sometimes set afire and left to run until they dropped. Six-guns and repeating rifles were well-suited to the grisly work, unlike the massacre of bison where high-powered, long-range weapons were required.

Fast Guns and Tin Stars

Our Civil War not only paved the way for swift expansion westward, but it also gave the West a brand-new breed of outlaw, hardened by four years of combat with no holds barred. Many were survivors of Confederate "irregular" brigades, like Quantrill's Raiders and the riotous troop led by George Todd. (Quantrill's right-hand man, before his death in 1864, was "Bloody Bill" Anderson, a psychopath who carried eight revolvers in his belt, along with a saber and a hatchet; four rifles were strapped on his horse, with two saddle bags crammed full of pistols.) Active Quantrill alumni during the post-war years included Frank and Jesse James, the Younger clan, and the high-riding Farrington Brothers.

In addition to common military background, many of the leading outlaws were related by blood or marriage, in the style of a frontier Mafia. The James brothers and the Youngers were cousins, and the Youngers were also related to the Dalton gang. Other outlaw family acts included the Sontag brothers, the Reno brothers (perpetrators of the first train robbery, in 1866), and the notorious Starr family. (To further complicate matters, Belle Starr, wife of Sam, produced an illegitimate child with Cole Younger.) Henry Starr, last of the venerable line, bridged the generation gap in 1914, swapping his horse for an automobile in the first mechanized flight from a bank robbery.

When cornered, Western outlaws waged ferocious battles with the marshals, vigilantes, and assorted townsmen who attempted to arrest them. The James-Younger gang's 1876 raid on Northfield, Minnesota, erupted into a bloody free-for-all lasting twenty minutes, effectively shattering the gang. Eight persons died at Coffeyville, Kansas, in 1892, when the Daltons tried to rob two banks simultaneously, and cannons were used the same year in an effort to breach outlaw Ned Christie's fortified stockade outside Tallequah, Oklahoma. When artillery failed, dynamite was employed, and Christie rode through the breach firing his Winchester repeater, toppled from the saddle by the mass fire of fifty rifles. A year later, at Ingalls, Oklahoma, three deputies were killed in a shootout with the Doolin gang, the outlaws literally escaping in the dust raised by flying bullets.

Frontier outlaws and lawmen alike favored six-guns, with Colt revolvers clearly the weapon of preference. Variations of the Colt '73 — dubbed the "Peacemaker" — were extremely popular, with 160,000 sold by 1898. The manufacturers recognized their new market west of the Mississippi, producing a "civilian" model with a 4.75-inch barrel, ideal for "fast draws." (The West's most famous single weapon was a Colt Peacemaker, serial number 139345, originally owned by Bill Hickok, with which he allegedly killed fourteen men in 1875 and 1876. After Hickok's death, his sister gave the weapon to a family friend, Pat Garrett, who used it to kill Billy the Kid in 1882.)

While Colts dominated the West, there were various other revolvers available. One, the Smith and Wesson Schofield, was a break-top model that ejected all six cartridges at once, thereby gaining a clear advantage over the Colts in terms of rapid reloading. Unfortunately, the Schofield's .45-caliber bullet was seated in a puny cartridge, containing 29 grains of black powder versus the Colt's 40 grains. Reduced range and accuracy were the result, and—in spite of their popularity with Jesse James and Cole Younger—the Schofields never attracted a serious following. Likewise, the excellent Remington Model 1875 Army revolver proved unpopular with frontiersmen, for reasons unknown, selling no more than 25,000 guns between 1875 and 1889.

As with revolvers, there was no "standard" caliber or cartridge in the West. The .45 was dominant, unquestionably boosted by its use in military side arms, and many gunmen favored the heavy projectile's knock-down power. Others, spending more time on the open range, opted for the .44-40 cartridge, simultaneously serving both their six-gun and the excellent Winchester '73 repeating rifle. Where size was concerned, quick-draw artists naturally favored shorter barrels for easy clearance, reserving longer-barreled weapons with their greater range and accuracy for distance work on the plains. Some two-gun types were known to wear the 4.75-inch "civilian" Colt on their right hip, ready for action, while sporting the heavier, 7.5-inch Cavalry model on their left.

One of the nineteenth century's most popular "alternative" pistols was the pepperbox, a short multibarreled weapon available in two basic styles. One model featured stationary barrels with a rotating firing pin, while in the other style the barrels rotated. Christian Sharps patented the best-selling pepperbox, a four-barrel model, in 1859, marketing 150,000 guns over the next two decades. Inaccurate beyond a few feet, the piece was still intimidating at close range, ideal for holdups and for settling disputes across a card table.

"Derringer" pistols were also widely used on both sides of the Mississippi, with Philadelphia gunsmith Henry Deringer, Jr., producing the first three-dollar model around 1850. Averaging four inches in length, most were single-shot weapons designed for easy concealment, a strong selling point with gamblers, dance hall girls, and any gunman who desired a hidden backup for his trusty Peacemaker. In contrast to their size, the stubby weapons were chambered for large cartridges, with .41 caliber being the norm, and they were deadly at close range. Once the guns caught on, large manufacturers gobbled up Deringer's design, adding a second "r" to disguise their flagrant thievery. Remington's double-barreled, over-under derringer was easily the most popular of all time, remaining in continuous production from 1865 until 1935.

Another common hide-out weapon, the "muff pistol," was so called because its diminutive size made it readily concealable inside a woman's muff or handbag. Muff pistols were the "Saturday night specials" of the nineteenth century, and they faced opposition from urban newspapers, falling into disrepute after editorials blamed firearm manufacturers for rising crime rates.

Another oddity, the "mob pistol," was a four-barreled flintlock, the loads discharging simultaneously with one squeeze of the trigger. Designed for crowd control, mob pistols saw widespread use in the East, during the riots of the Jacksonian era, later making their way to California by ship, as nervous captains armed themselves against potential mutineers. Such weapons clearly violated the classic gunfighter's "code of the West," but California — then, as now — was a world apart, and mob pistols were a welcome addition to the white man's arsenal, and were used in slaughtering Chinese and Mexicans around the lawless mining camps.

Regardless of their hardware, Western outlaws were rarely the crack shots portrayed by Hollywood. Jesse James, a legendary pistol fighter in his teenage days with Quantrill's Raiders, once shot off the tip of his own finger while cleaning a six-gun. On another occasion, he squeezed off six shots at an unarmed bank teller, firing at close range, and missed each time. Black powder, with its swirling clouds of smoke, undoubtedly contributed to Jesse's embarrassment, but the fact remains that few outlaws qualified as expert marksmen.

A fine line divided frontier lawmen from their lawless adversaries, and many "tin stars" played both sides of the game with fine impartiality. Wide-open communities, in search of a hair-trigger "town tamer," were seldom inclined to question their savior's background — or his shady off-duty behavior. In fact, one man's marshal was another's hired killer, as in Dodge City, where a local newspaper described Wyatt Earp as a man "famous in the cheerful business of depopulating the county."

Wild Bill Hickok—sometimes labeled "Duck Bill" by detractors—was charged with murder in 1861, after ambushing three unarmed farmers in Nebraska. The charges were ultimately dismissed, clearing the way for Hickok's career in Western law enforcement, but he remained notorious for his corruption and involvement with organized gambling. In October 1871, Hickok killed gambler Phil Coe in a dispute concerning the death of a stray dog, then shot one of his own deputies who came to investigate the gunfire. (The dog in question had been shot by Coe, depriving Hickok of his standard 25-cent bounty.)

Another lethal lawman, Steve Long, killed eight men during two months of service as a deputy marshal in Laramie, Wyoming. In October 1867, he waded into a street fight with both guns blazing, mortally wounding five of the eight unarmed combatants. A year later, while moonlighting as a highway robber, Long was captured and unceremoniously hanged by vigilantes.

Around Dodge City, Wyatt Earp and Bat Masterson were known as "the fighting pimps," in reference to their protection of the local bawdy houses. In 1880, the Earp brothers descended on Tombstone, supported by lethal Doc Holliday, their arrival sparking immediate conflict with the resident Clanton-McLowery gang. The rivalry climaxed in thirty seconds of mayhem at the O.K. Corral, followed by a series of ambush slayings, with various Clanton adherents riddled while "resisting arrest."

A deadly reputation often served the Western lawman where his skill with firearms might have left him bleeding in the street. Bill Hickok was an adequate shot—once dropping childhood acquaintance Dave Tutt at 75 yards—but most of his exploits were apocryphal, with tales generated by Hickok himself. (By 1870, his ambush of three Nebraska farmers had become a stand-up fight against "the McCanles gang," with Hickok killing nine desperadoes single-handed.) Bat Masterson, one of three gun-slinging brothers who worked both sides of the law, was credited with killing 31 men by 1884; in fact, he killed only one in his life, and that after Masterson was gravely wounded by his assailant.

When frontier marshals drew their guns, they were most likely to "buffalo" their prisoners, described by one practitioner as "the gentle art of bending a revolver barrel around a lawbreaker's skull." As practiced by the likes of Earp and Hickok, "buffaloing" amounted to no more than police brutality, with victims typically disarmed and in custody before they were beaten. Wyatt Earp especially enjoyed slugging cowboys, gloating over the fact in his memoirs. "As practically every prisoner heaved into the calaboose was thoroughly buffaloed in the process," Earp wrote, "we made quite a dent in cowboy conceit." Earp's zeal led rancher Tobe Driskill to place a thousand-dollar bounty on the marshal's head, but no one managed to collect the prize.

A weapon perfectly designed for "crowning" cowboys was the "Buntline Special," a Colt .45 with 12-inch barrel presented by dime novelist E.Z.C. Johnson — alias "Ned Buntline" — to some of his favorite lawmen. According to Wyatt Earp, the awkward piece never hampered his draw, but other recipients — notably Bat Masterson and Bill Tilghman — sawed the barrel off to the standard 7.5-inch length of the Colt Cavalry model.

Shotguns came into their own as antipersonnel weapons during the latter half of the nineteenth century, used widely by outlaws and lawmen alike. Devastating at close range, double-barreled "scatterguns" were ideal for sudden-death confrontations, repeatedly proving their value in the defense (or the robbery) of stagecoaches and trains. Doc Holliday used a sawed-off shotgun to kill Tom McLowery at the O.K. Corral, forsaking his favorite Colt in the heat of the moment. Train robbers Rube Barrow and Sam Ketchum were both killed by shotgun guards in the 1890s, while outlaw Jack Davis was vaporized by two blasts in the face, his unrecognizable condition sparking rumors that an underling died in his place, the *real* Davis escaping to relax with stolen gold in Nicaragua.

High Noon

In 1855, a California judge named William Gwin squared off against an adversary, Joe McCorkle, for a stand-up shooting staged some distance from the judge's home. A thoughtful man, Gwin made arrangements for a mounted messenger to keep his wife informed of progress in the duel.

Galloping up to the house that morning, the messenger proclaimed, "The first fire has been exchanged and no one is hurt."

"Thank God!" cried Mrs. Gwin.

In time, the rider came again, announcing, "The second fire has been exchanged and no one is hurt."

To which a grateful Mrs. Gwin replied, "Praised be the Lord."

Once more the messenger rode back and forth, reporting, "The third fire has been exchanged and no one is hurt."

"That's good," said Mrs. Gwin.

Upon his fourth appearance at the house, the messenger was asked to stay for supper. As they finished off dessert, he said, "Oh, by the way, the fourth fire has been exchanged and no one is hurt. What do you think of that, Mrs. Gwin?"

"I think," she replied, "that there has been some mighty poor shooting."

In contrast to the Western myth enshrined by Hollywood, poor shooting was the rule of thumb in frontier showdowns. Rowdy Joe Lowe once traded fifty shots with an adversary before finally dropping his man in Delano, Kansas, and the case is not unique. In April 1879, Levi Richardson fired five shots at Cockeyed Frank Loving, missing five times in the smoky atmosphere of Dodge City's Long Branch Saloon; Loving wasted three shots in return, before finally killing Richardson at a range of two feet. Three years later, Cockeye exchanged sixteen shots with opponent Jack Allen, and no one was hit. (Loving's luck ran out the next day, during a replay in which he was killed.)

Self-styled expert Wyatt Earp once described gunfighting as the art of "going into action with the greatest speed of which a man's muscles are capable, but mentally unflustered by an urge to hurry or the need for complicated nervous and muscular actions which trick shooting involves." In short, while speed was certainly desirable, it would not do the trick without a fair degree of accuracy in the bargain.

In 1876, Turkey Creek Johnson provided a perfect example of grace under pressure, confronting two gunmen at once. Johnson's enemies opened up at a range of fifty yards, squeezing off six rounds apiece without scoring a hit on their target. At thirty yards, Johnson took aim and killed one of his adversaries with a single shot, the survivor wasting three more rounds before a second bullet dropped him in his tracks.

Psychological warfare was also useful, if properly employed. In 1889, at Carson City, a small town in Colorado, Red Ivan and Pedro Arondondo felt obliged to shoot it out over an accusation of cheating at cards. Ivan requested some time to prepare, buying himself a black suit for the occasion, moving on from there to order a headstone with the inscription: "Pedro Arondondo, born 1857 — died 1889, from a bullet wound between the eyes fired by Red Ivan." It worked.

There *were* some classic gunslicks in the West, but passing time has sanitized their reputations and inflated body counts until the truth is difficult, if not impossible, to ascertain. Most professional "shootists" were no more than common murderers, willing to back-shoot whenever they could, and some — like alcoholic Clay Allison, who once shot a bunkmate for snoring — would doubtless be classified as psychotic serial killers today. Luke Short, "the undertaker's friend," was a charter member of the Earp-Masterson "Dodge City gang," who killed at least six men in defense of his bootlegging trade with the Indians. Wild Bill Longley, a pathological racist, killed an estimated 30 blacks before he was finally hanged, for shooting a white man, in 1877. As undisputed leader of the pack, boasting 44 kills, Texan John Wesley Hardin was one of the few gunmen to actually carry a notched weapon. (Years later, after retiring to New York City as a sportswriter, Bat Masterson kept up a thriving trade in "genuine" notched Colts.)

When speed was mandatory, Western gunmen used a variety of techniques to get the job done. Most tied their holsters down, with leather thongs around their thighs, and some greased the interior to shave a few microseconds off the draw. The front sights of revolvers were often filed down to prevent them from snagging at critical moments, and triggers were wired back on occasion, permitting rapid fire by means of "fanning" the hammer with the gunman's free hand.

A gunfighter's speed might depend on the way that he carried his gun, but no two professionals seemed to agree on the proper technique. Some wore holsters high on their hips, while others tied them low on the thigh; others favored a cross-hand draw, with pistols worn reversed, butts forward. Shoulder holsters were rarely fast enough for head-on confrontations, but they might be useful for back-up weapons. Derringers were often concealed inside hats or boots, sometimes spring-loaded up a gunman's sleeve. Gunslinger Frank Leslie wore his revolver in a special quick-fire rig, attached by a stud to a slotted plate on his gunbelt, fired by swiveling from the hip without the traditional draw. (He also used his wife for target practice, tracing her outline with bullets on the walls at home!)

Pure trickery played a role in many shootouts, with gunmen choosing their position to place the sun in an opponent's eyes, or taking a leaf from Bill Hickok's book and throwing their hat in an adversary's face. The "border roll," also dubbed the "road agent's spin," was employed as a show of surrender, offering pistols butt-foremost, with a finger through the trigger-guard, spinning the weapon back into a firing grip at the last instant. John Wesley Hardin once used the border roll to embarrass Marshal Hickok in Abilene, but it took skill and practice to keep from dropping the gun, with disastrous results.

By 1895, the best-known gunmen of the West were either dead, or else retired—like Earp and Masterson—to other fields of enterprise. A few odd specimens, like Shotgun Bill McKinney, would carry their act into the new century, but time and the odds were against them. History had turned another page, and the history of firearms technology was being written on foreign battlefields.

F O U R
AMERICA AT WAR

Ironically, despite a history replete with martial conflict, the United States traditionally has been slow to arm herself as war clouds gather, hasty in disposal of her weapons once a momentary threat has been eliminated. Conservatism carried to the point of willful negligence prevented U.S. arsenals from keeping up with new advances in technology throughout the latter nineteenth century, with the result that Yankee soldiers found themselves ill trained and ill equipped for combat on the modern battlefield.

While the United States was waging ruthless war on aborigines at home, innovations overran the field of European arms. A Frenchman, M. Vieille, invented smokeless powder during 1884, attempting to eliminate the telltale clouds of gunsmoke that betrayed his country's riflemen to enemies in battle. He succeeded brilliantly, developing a new propellant with chemical and ballistic stability far exceeding the best of black powders, banishing gunsmoke while simultaneously permitting higher projectile velocities without excessive pressure.

New propellant, in turn, required new bullets, as traditional lead projectiles began to disintegrate in flight, and the solution was already waiting in the wings. A Swiss officer, Major Bode, had developed the first *jacketed* projectile in 1875, surrounding the lead core with a layer of copper, producing bullets that were lighter, longer, and more accurate at greater range.

Another breakthrough, in 1884, was Hiram Maxim's invention of automatic weapons, utilizing recoil pressures to eject spent cartridges and chamber new rounds at high speed. Maxim's weapons were the first "machine guns" — as opposed to manually operated weapons like the Gatling — and British troops placed their first official orders in 1887. A new age of warfare was looming on the horizon, and the United States was lagging sadly behind her potential enemies in firearms technology.

The "Splendid Little War"

By 1890, America's Army was the only major military force on earth still armed with single-shot rifles. European forces had shifted to magazine-loaded repeaters during the 1880s, but members of the U.S. Ordnance Board were slow in catching on to modern trends. In 1890, they bypassed the excellent Mauser designs, selecting the Norwegian Krag-Jorgensen rifle for American troops, putting the weapon through various modifications before its official acceptance in 1892. Ignoring the advent of smokeless powder, America's new bolt-action magazine rifles were chambered for the .30-40 Krag black powder cartridge, thereby placing troops at further risk each time they pulled a trigger.

In 1896, Krags had been issued only to America's 27,000 regular troops. Another 400,000 would be manufactured by 1898, but in the meantime some 200,000 volunteers and members of assorted state militia units would be marching off to battle armed with single-shot weapons, the same .45-70 antiques that had served in the Indian wars.

A rare concession to modern technology was made in adopting the Colt-Browning Model 1895 machine gun, developed by American inventor John M. Browning from designs begun in 1889. With Hiram Maxim's guns already working on the recoil principle, Browning tried a new tack, tapping gases from the weapon's barrel to power a piston-and-lever arrangement mounted beneath the receiver. Nicknamed the "potato digger" for the motion of its outer mechanism, Browning's gun was chambered for the .30-caliber Krag cartridge, devouring belted ammunition at a cyclic rate of 400 to 500 rounds per minute.

American Marines would use John Browning's gun in Cuba during 1898, but for the most part, soldiers on the line would still be cranking up their Gatling "coffee grinders" and the larger Hotchkiss guns. Black powder was the order of the day, with grim results. At El Caney, the smoke produced by U.S. rifles granted Spanish snipers, with their smokeless Mausers, perfect opportunity to zero in on their Yankee targets, breaking the American assault. At San Juan Hill it was the same, with 15,000 U.S. troops sustaining 1,400 casualties in their attempt to rout a garrison of 700 Spaniards. The heroic "charge" was actually a slogging crawl through deadly sniper fire, with heavy fire from Gatling guns at last required to drive the Spaniards from their trenches.

Madrid's concession of defeat in 1898 brought no cease-fire for the United States. Initially receptive to America's removal of the Spanish yoke, proud Filipinos seemed less grateful once they understood the Yankees planned to stay, perhaps forever. Eighty thousand native rebels joined Emilio Aquinaldo's February 1899 revolt, providing the United States with an uncanny four-year preview of the war in Vietnam.

Outnumbered four to one, the Yankee soldiers learned to deal with Moro tribesmen, high on drugs and the delusion of their own invincibility, who would attack a Gatling gun with spears and bolo knives. Against such fervor—like policemen of another generation, faced with suspects "wired" on PCP—the troopers found their Krags inadequate. Their side arms were Colt Model 1892 double-action revolvers, easy to load with their new swing-out cylinders, but the .38 Long Colt cartridge lacked the stopping power of the old single-action .45s.

In desperation, the army turned to shotguns, marking the first military use of such weapons with its adoption of the Winchester Model 1897, a slide-action (pump-style) weapon chambered for the mighty 12-gauge, sporting a 20-inch barrel that made it ideal for close encounters in the Philippine jungles.

Lessons learned in battle—and from tests performed on captured Spanish weapons — led to changes in the U.S. arsenal from 1900 onward. Building on the superior Mauser design of bolt-action rifles, America's Springfield armory first produced an inefficient .30-caliber model in 1900, improving it over time to create the famous Model 1903 — dubbed the "Springfield" — which was issued to regular troops during 1904 and 1905. Future modifications would alter the Springfield to chamber the new U.S. 1906 Model cartridge in .30 caliber, now famous worldwide as the ".30-06" ("thirty-ought-six").

The Ordnance Board had learned one crucial lesson from the Philippine campaign in terms of handgun stopping-power. In 1909, the army adopted Colt's New Service revolver in .45 caliber, prompting Smith and Wesson to develop their own competitive model. Both were double-action revolvers with the "new" swing-out cylinder designed to facilitate swift reloading, and the increased muzzle velocity of their projectiles — 830 feet per second versus the .38 Long Colt's 750 fps — gave shooters a fair edge on dropping their targets the first time around.

"Over There"

By the time America involved herself in World War I, three years of grim attrition had firmly established the new terms of modern combat. Machine guns had frozen the front lines, dictating the style of trench warfare and chalking up awesome body counts as soldiers went "over the top," mounting obsolete traditional charges across "no-man's land." Rifles were still issued as the infantry soldier's primary weapon, but bayonets and gun butts were more useful in the trenches, where weeks of tedium were climaxed in moments of panicky hand-to-hand combat. Both sides would strive to break the stalemate — Germany launching the first poison gas attacks in April 1915, Britain introducing tanks a year later — but Americans arriving "over there" in 1917 would find the static killing ground essentially unchanged.

Because machine guns so completely dominated World War I — both on the land and, later, in the air — their several types and tactics of deployment rate discussion here. Operating on the recoil principle (like Maxim's gun) or by the pressure of expanding gas (like Browning's), the machine gun is an *automatic* weapon; simply put, it will continue firing while the trigger is depressed, until its ammunition is expended, or mechanical malfunction causes it to jam. Conversely, *semiautomatic* weapons, while employing the same recoil or gas-operated principle, require a distinct and separate depression of the trigger every time a single round is fired. (The standard "automatic pistol" is, in fact, a semiautomatic weapon.)

Machine guns typically are designated by their size and special function. Heavy machine guns are chambered for cartridges of .50 caliber or larger, employed in fortified positions or mounted on various vehicles. Medium machine guns — commonly referred to simply as "machine guns" — weigh between 25 and 60 pounds, firing standard rifle cartridges from a belt, drum, or box magazine. The standard machine gun of World War I, medium models were typically mounted on tripods, protected by earthworks and sand bags, controlling a broad field of fire to the front. Deprived of true mobility by weight and the necessity of keeping extra ammunition close at hand, they were (and are) primarily defensive weapons, useless to a soldier charging over open ground against an enemy position.

The solution, after 1915, was the introduction of the light machine gun, fairly portable at a weight of 15 to 30 pounds, providing mobile firepower to infantry attack units. Chambered for the same rifle cartridge as the medium machine gun, lighter weapons were normally fed from box or drum magazines, eliminating the cumbersome belt feed. Customarily fitted with a buttstock like a standard rifle, the light machine gun normally features a folding bipod or other convenient support for the muzzle.

In time, as aircraft and machine guns proliferated together, pilots inevitably began shooting at one another. From their intended role as observers or "scouts," the new breed of airmen quickly became full-fledged combatants, blazing away with rifles and handguns (including semiautomatic pistols fitted with extended magazines and brass-catchers to retrieve spent casings). Next, machine guns were mounted on the topmost wings of biplanes, but their accuracy left much to be desired. Attempts to mount machine guns on the forward cowling of an aircraft were disastrous, with pilots literally shooting off their own propellers, until Dutch inventor Anthony Fokker managed to synchronize guns and props in 1915. Fokkers were the terror of the European skies until a few were downed in action, and the Allies had a chance to steal the mechanism for themselves.

Members of the American Expeditionary Force in Europe entered the trenches armed with the Model 1903 bolt-action rifle. A .30-caliber bolt-action, fed by a five-round box magazine, the "Springfield" measured 43.2 inches overall and weighed 8.69 pounds. The weapon's intermediate length—somewhere between a standard rifle and the shorter carbine—provided excellent balance. The old '03s are still prized by serious marksmen. A later variation, the Model 1903 Mk 1, was modified to accommodate the ill-conceived Pedersen Device, replacing the standard bolt with a new receiver firing special .30-caliber pistol ammunition, fed through an overhead magazine, striving toward production of the first crude assault rifle. Issued too late for widespread use at the front, the Mk 1 was held in reserve for the anticipated 1919 offensive, which never took place.

Our British Allies in the "War to End All Wars" were armed with Lee-Enfield rifles in .303 caliber, fed by a ten-round detachable box magazine. The Lee-Enfield's bolt action was weak on safety features, in comparison with the Mauser design [Chapter 5], but it was fast and easy to operate. Measuring 44.6 inches overall, the British weapon hurled its jacketed bullets down range at a velocity of 2,080 feet per second.

Frenchmen in the trenches used an older, longer rifle, measuring 51.3 inches from muzzle to butt. Designated the Lebel 1886/93—with numerals denoting the year of design and its most recent modification—this was an 8mm (.315-caliber) bolt-action weapon, fed by an eight-round tubular magazine. A secondary French weapon, the Mousqueton Berthier carbine, was also chambered in 8mm, feeding its load from a small three-round box magazine. In combat, the carbine's short 18-inch barrel seemed dwarfed by attachment of a fearsome bayonet.

World War I was the last major conflict in which pistols served as a primary infantry weapon. Trench warfare meant killing at close range, where bayonets, clubbed rifles, and brass-knuckle "trench knives" were more useful than finely tuned weapons sighted in at 1,000 yards. For once, Americans were on top of the game, having adopted the powerful .45-caliber Colt "automatic" pistol (designed by John Browning) in 1911. Operating on the recoil principle, this classic man-stopper carried seven rounds in a box magazine, inserted through the butt of the pistol grip. The big Colts proved themselves along the Rio Grande with General Pershing, tracking Pancho Villa, and there were 55,553 on hand when America entered the European war. Another 450,000 were manufactured prior to the armistice, but supply could never keep pace with demand, and U.S. forces also used the older Colt or Smith and Wesson .45 revolvers.

British troops in World War I used a variety of side arms, all chambered for the heavy .455-caliber bullet (actually .441 caliber). The chief weapons in service were the big Webley revolvers, described by some aficionados as the toughest and most accurate handguns ever made. Be that as it may, the Webleys *were* extremely powerful, with the ability to function well in filth. Officers of the Royal Navy and Royal Marines were issued Webley & Scott self-loading (semiautomatic) pistols, carrying seven of the big .455 rounds in a box magazine, but poor exterior design made the weapons uncomfortable to fire, and they never achieved the popularity of the Webley revolvers.

One curious side arm introduced during the war was the Webley Fosbery "automatic revolver." On firing, recoil drove the barrel, cylinder, and top frame back along a slide, above the butt, cocking the hammer before a return spring drove the mechanism back to its original position. On the return trip, an angled stud in the slide ran through a machined groove in the revolver's cylinder, producing rotation. Awkward in combat, since the sliding action roughly doubled an already substantial recoil, the Webley Fosbery made history as the only major twentieth-century revolver equipped with a safety mechanism.

The standard side arm for French officers in World War I was the Lebel revolver, an 8mm double-action weapon notable as the first European revolver boasting a swing-out cylinder. The Lebel's cartridges were seriously underpowered, unlikely to drop a man with one shot unless vital organs were penetrated, but troops still favored the piece for its reliability in rugged combat conditions.

Shotguns continued in use with American troops overseas, with the venerable Winchester Model 1897 serving as the dough-boy's standard "trench broom." Modified to take a bayonet, the

Winchesters were supplemented by the Remington M-10, a 12-gauge pump-action gun holding five rounds in its tubular magazine. In all, 40,000 shotguns were purchased by the U.S. government in World War I, and many of them made it to the trenches, where they served their users well.

The Colt-Browning Model 1895 machine gun was considered obsolete in 1917, and while some specimens made the journey to France, few saw action at the front. Their replacement was the Browning Model 1917, a .30-caliber weapon employing the "short recoil" system, wherein recoil pushes the barrel and breechblock to the rear of the gun, chambering a new round after each shot. Sporting a pistol grip and conventional trigger, unlike the dual spade grips on British Vickers guns, the belt-fed Browning '17 fired at a cyclic rate of 450 to 600 rounds per minute. To prevent barrel melt-down, the weapons were water cooled, with a special sleeve surrounding the barrel. Rushed into production with America's declaration of war against Germany, 68,000 Brownings were manufactured by November 1918.

The Browning Automatic Rifle was America's attempt to bridge the gap between a standard rifle and a light machine gun. Weighing in at sixteen pounds and firing at a cyclic rate of 550 rounds per minute, the BAR was demonstrated for military leaders in 1917, with production beginning a year later. It would reach the trenches in September 1918, its rugged construction and intimidating appearance compensating for the limited firepower of its 20-round box magazine.

Britain's standard machine gun in World War I was the Vickers gun, a .303-caliber modification of the original Maxim design, which entered military service in 1907. Belt-fed and mounted on a heavy tripod, the Vickers fired at a cyclic rate of 450 to 500 rounds per minute. In the early models, steam was vented from the barrel's water jacket, but in combat, rising clouds of vapor marked the gun's location for enemy return fire. An improved condensation system was designed, siphoning steam away from the barrel by hose. (An air-cooled model of the Vickers was designed for use on aircraft, later in the war.)

An international curiosity, the Lewis gun was invented by American Samuel Maclean but first produced in Europe, after a model designed by Col. Isaac Lewis. Adopted by the Belgian army as a light machine gun during 1913, the Lewis was later manufactured in Britain for use by the Allies, including American troops. Chambered in .303 caliber, the bulky piece fired at a cyclic rate of 450 to 500 rounds per minute, feeding ammunition from 47- and 97-round overhead drums. The Lewis gun was gas operated, with a complex inner mechanism prone to jamming even under careful maintenance, and delicate drum magazines that were a source of continual problems. The weapon's barrel was enclosed in an air-cooling jacket using the forced draught system, and the overrated system was abandoned for mounting the weapon on aircraft. For all of its shortcomings, the Lewis gun still takes honors as the first of the true light machine guns, its shoulder stock and relatively light weight (27 pounds) breaking new ground in the field of mobility.

French troops in World War I were armed with various Hotchkiss machine guns, chambered in 8mm. The predominant Model 1914 was a heavy, gas-operated weapon with curious "doughnut" cooling rings around its barrel, capable of firing at a cyclic rate between 400 and 600 rounds per minute. The Model '14 devoured ammunition in 24- and 30-round strips, alternately feeding on 249-round strips, arranged in three-round links. When the Hotchkiss '14 was unavailable, commanders brought the Model 1909 out of mothballs, achieving cyclic fire rates of 500 rounds per minute with the curious 30-round metal strip feed system.

The war's worst automatic weapon was the French Cauchat, produced in 1915 as a light machine gun, foisted off on the Americans in a flagrant example of war profiteering. Poorly designed, with a curved 20-round magazine underneath the receiver, the Cauchat was awkward to handle and subject to frequent malfunctions. Even so, the U.S. Army was persuaded to purchase 16,000 of the guns in 8mm, placing a second order for 19,000 in .30 caliber, with "improved" vertical box magazines. In fact, the improvements were illusory, and the more powerful American cartridge produced even more frequent failures in combat.

World War II and Korea

More than any other war in history, the global conflict known as World War II was a transitional experience for members of the common infantry. The vast majority of soldiers called to fight from

1939 to 1941 were trained with old bolt-action rifles dating from the First World War, and many carried the antiques to combat. By the closing days in 1945, most fighting men had seen a preview of the future, with proliferation of the semiautomatic arms and submachine guns that were ancestors of the modern assault rifle.

The United States, uncharacteristically, had cast herself in the role of pioneer by adopting the M1 rifle, designed by John Garand, in 1932. The first self-loading (semiautomatic) rifle accepted for military service, the M1 Garand was a gas-operated weapon weighing 9.5 pounds. Chambered in .30 caliber, its eight-round magazine was loaded with metal clips full of cartridges, inserted through the top of the receiver. In practice, this meant that a rifleman had to reload his weapon with eight rounds or nothing, making it impossible to "top off" a partial load. A further problem was experienced upon ejection of the empty clip, producing a distinctive sound to mark the rifleman's position for his enemies. But overall the new M1 was rugged, accurate, and popular with front-line troops.

It took some time for the Garand to reach production after its acceptance by the military, but most regular troops had received their M1s by December 1941. Following Pearl Harbor, mass enlistments and conscription far outstripped production, and thousands of 1903 Springfields were dusted off to take up the slack. By the end of the war, 5.5 million Garands had been manufactured for use at the front, effectively removing America from the bolt-action era forever.

In 1940, army spokesmen voiced specific interest in a lightweight carbine for use by support troops and rear-echelon personnel. The resultant product, dubbed the Carbine M1, was unique in its use of special cartridge, designed as a compromise between pistol and rifle ammunition. (Standard carbines fire a normal rifle cartridge.) Although it lacked the big Garand's stopping power — with a muzzle velocity of 1,970 feet per second versus the full-sized M1's 2,805 fps — many troops preferred the 5.2-pound carbine, with its 15- and 30-round magazines. The weapon quickly found its place in front-line units, serving extensively with U.S. Marines in the Pacific. Subsequent variant models included the M1A1 (with folding stock, for airborne units), the M2 (full-automatic, with a cyclic rate of 750 to 775 rounds per minute), and the M3 night-fighter (with bulky infrared sight). In all, 6,332,000 M1 carbines were manufactured during the war, making this the most prolific weapon in the Pacific theater.

British troops in World War II continued using the sturdy Lee-Enfield bolt-action rifles, modified to reduce the cost and time of manufacturing. Designated the Rifle No. 4 Mark I, the "new" weapon still fed its .303-caliber rounds from a ten-round box magazine. A jungle version, produced after September 1944 and dubbed the Rifle No. 5 Mk I, was the same basic weapon with barrel length reduced to 18.75 inches (from the No. 4's original 25.2 inches). A shorter barrel means more recoil and muzzle flash, so the short No. 5 came equipped with a rubber butt pad and a conical flash-hider attached to its muzzle.

Our Soviet allies made an early move toward innovative self-loading rifles with the Tokarev SVT38, a gas-operated weapon adopted for service in 1938. Poor internal design led to frequent breakdowns, and the weapon was replaced two years later by an improved SVT40. Chambered in 7.62mm, fed from a 10-round box magazine, the rifle weighed 8.58 pounds fully loaded. Its fierce recoil and muzzle blast were reduced by addition of a muzzle brake with open ports to channel the escaping gases.

In the realm of side arms, battlefield experience in World War I had led to minor alterations of the Colt M1911, primarily concerned with the mainspring housing, the hammer spur, and grip safety configuration. The revised model, designated M1911A1, remained the standard U.S. military pistol until 1985, when it was finally replaced. In addition to standard .45-caliber ammunition, World War II saw the introduction of tracer rounds and "high density" shot shells. The latter were designed for pilots downed in combat, so they could shoot fish and game, but the steel pellets were equally effective against humans, and their survival function soon faded into the background.

British forces continued to use revolvers through the Second World War, but the heavy .455-caliber models had been phased out after 1919, and replaced with a lighter .38-caliber cartridge. Two pistols resulted from the change, and both were widely used. Designated the Enfield No. 2 Mk 1 and the Webley Mk 4, both were double-action arms with five-inch barrels, weighing 1.7 pounds apiece. Demand required that Britain supplement her own production with purchase of overseas models, and large orders were placed for the .38-caliber Smith and Wesson, variously dubbed the Revolver .38/200 or Revolver No. 2 Caliber .380.

Soviet troops likewise entered the war armed with six-guns, but they made the shift to semiautomatic weapons in midstream. The Nagant Model 1895 was a 7.62mm revolver manufactured in Russia from its date of invention through 1940, produced in both single- and double-action models. (Czarist policy, enforcing class distinctions, issued the double-action pistols to officers, while the slower single-action weapons were provided to enlisted men.) The Nagant's curious design attempted to eliminate the leakage of pro-pellant gas between the weapon's cylinder and barrel, ramming the cylinder forward on firing to close the tiny gap (known as "head space"). The mechanism required a special cartridge, boasting a fully recessed bullet, and stands as one of the more peculiar re-volver designs in modern history.

The Nagant's gradual replacement, designated the Tokarev TT-33, was a Soviet version of the Colt-Browning pistols, operating on the same recoil principle as the American M1911. Wartime production never caught up with demand, and many Nagant re-volvers remained in the field, but Tokarevs became the standard Soviet side arm of the post-war era. Chambered in 7.62mm with an eight-round magazine, the TT-33 measured 4.57 inches overall, compared to the Colt's 8.6 inches; it was also considerably lighter, at 1.83 pounds versus the Colt's three-pound heft, and its muzzle velocity far surpassed the .45's, at 1,380 fps versus 825 fps.

Without trenches to sweep, military shotguns returned to their original function as jungle weapons during World War II. American troops in the Pacific still used the Winchester M1897, modified with a new take-down feature, a Parkerized (antirust) finish, and a reinforced buttstock. The existing supply was supple-mented by more recent Winchester, Remington, Stevens, and Ith-aca models, with the Remington M11 "riot gun" seeing widespread action. In the Pacific, shotguns were used for jungle fighting, guarding prisoners, and clearing out Japanese strongpoints, as in the fortified dwellings of Garapan, on Saipan. (British also made limited use of shotguns during the Burma campaign and elsewhere, but never in numbers to equal American issue.)

Machine guns in the second global conflict never held the

prominence they enjoyed in World War I, since tactics were more flexible, relying on mobility and speed epitomized by Hitler's *blitz-krieg*. Despite the changing times, however, automatic arms were still efficient killers, and the changing face of war produced a host of new designs.

America's heavy machine gun was the Browning .50-caliber model, introduced in 1921. Measuring 65 inches overall and weighing in at 84 pounds (on a 44-pound tripod), the weapon was a prodigious killing machine, spewing bullets at a cyclic rate of 450 to 575 rounds per minute, with a stunning muzzle velocity of 2,900 feet per second. Armor-piercing rounds were also available, and the big Brownings were often deployed for antiaircraft duties on the M45 Maxson Mount, with four guns mounted together for massed fire.

A number of water-cooled Browning M1917s saw action in World War II, but they were gradually replaced by air-cooled weapons in the M1919 series. Most widespread was the M1919A4, with 438,971 produced during four years of combat. Chambered in .30 caliber, the standard piece weighed 31 pounds, firing at a cyclic rate of 400 to 500 rounds per minute. Variant forms included the M1919A5 (designed for tanks), the M2 (an air force model, featuring both fixed wing and flexible installations), and the AN-M2 (utilized by naval forces).

The Browning Automatic Rifle played an active role in World War II, with some revisions based on battlefield experience. The BAR M1918A1 had a bipod affixed to the muzzle, for better support, while the M1918A2 featured bipod modifications and a brace on the shoulder stock, providing greater stability. The finished product weighed in at 19.4 pounds, with a loaded 20-round magazine, and it possessed flexible rates of fire, ranging from 500 to 600 rounds per minute (fast rate) to 300 or 400 rpm (slow rate).

The Vickers Mk 1 machine gun remained standard for British troops after World War I, chambered in .303 caliber, weighing 40 pounds with a full water jacket (and mounting a 48.5-pound tripod), with a cyclic rate of fire between 450 and 500 rounds per minute. Several modified versions had surfaced by 1939, including the heavy Mk 4 and Mk 5 in .50 caliber. By 1943, introduction of the Mark 8Z boat-tailed bullet gave the Vickers gun an awesome killing range of 4,500 yards.

Britain's Vickers-Berthier light machine guns evolved from pre-World War I French designs, with the Mk 3 weighing in at 24.4 pounds, spitting its .303-caliber projectiles from a 30-round box magazine at a cyclic rate of 450 to 600 rounds per minute. The Vickers G.O. Gun (gas-operated) was even lighter, at 21 pounds, feeding cartridges from a 96-round drum at the sizzling rate of 1,000 rounds per minute. Both weapons featured a shoulder stock, pistol grip, and a bipod to support the muzzle.

Soviet troops used a full range of machine guns in combat, topping the line with the heavy DShK1938, in .50 caliber. Mounted on a stout wheeled carriage, the piece weighed 73.5 pounds and devoured its ammunition belts at a rate of 550 to 600 rounds per minute. The Soviet medium machine gun was designated SG43, for its year of introduction; chambered in 7.62mm, it weighed 30.4 pounds and fired at a cyclic rate of 500 to 640 rounds per minute. Russia's light machine gun, the Degtyerev DP Model 1928, resembled the British Vickers-Berthier in outline, feeding from a large overhead drum magazine. Simple and tough, designed to withstand rough treatment and brutal weather, it is still in use today by various guerrilla bands around the world.

A relatively new design, the *submachine gun*, took mobility a long stride further during World War II, providing individual soldiers with lightweight fully automatic weapons. Designed to chamber pistol ammunition, submachine guns had been pioneered, without much real success, by Italy and Germany in World War I. [See Chapter 5.] Most use the "blowback" system, where a trigger pull releases the breechblock to move forward under power from a large spring, stipping a cartridge from the feed and thrusting it into the chamber for firing, after which recoil drives the block and spring back to their original position. Limited range in submachine guns was generally balanced by their mobility and high rate of fire.

American General John Thompson had begun work on a full-auto "trench broom" in 1918, but the war ended before he produced a functional weapon. There was little military interest in the 1919 or 1921 model Thompsons, with their detachable stocks and vertical foregrips, but some of the weapons saw action with U.S. Marines in China and Nicaragua during the late 1920s and early 1930s. Chambered in .45 caliber, the "Tommy gun" was built to handle 20- or 30-round box magazines, in addition to circular 50-

and 100-round drums, with early models firing at a cyclic rate of some 800 rounds per minute.

The U.S. Navy placed an order for Thompsons in 1927, requesting certain modifications that gave birth to the Model 1928, sporting a new horizontal forearm (in place of the pistol grip) and a reduced rate of fire (650 rpm). The army started ordering in 1939, stocking up on another 2 million guns between 1940 and 1944. Many of those were the remodeled M1, featuring a relocated cocking bolt and a receiver that would only take the vertical box magazines. (The larger drums were bulky and the general staff regarded them as too complex for average soldiers.) An M1 Thompson was a no-frills weapon weighing 10.45 pounds with loaded magazine in place, and it achieved a cyclic rate of 700 rounds per minute.

Other American submachine guns included the Reising M50, introduced in 1940, with 100,000 manufactured by war's end. Lighter than the Tommy gun at 8.16 pounds, the Reising fired at a cyclic rate of 550 rounds per minute, feeding 12- and 20-round box magazines, but its many failures led to ultimate rejection by the Marine Corps. An "improved" model, the M55, proved no more successful in action.

Cheaper yet, the M3 "grease guns" were all metal, with most of their parts stamped out by machine. Weighing in at 10.25 pounds, with a telescopic wire butt, the M3 used a 30-round box magazine, achieving cyclic rates of fire between 350 and 450 rounds per minute. Major drawbacks included the rudimentary sights, an ejection port covered by a hinged flap, a flimsy cocking handle poorly situated on the weapon's right side, and the total absence of a safety mechanism. Troops universally preferred the Tommy gun, but thousands were compelled to settle for the M3 as the only submachine gun currently available.

Britain's version of the "grease gun" was the Sten 9mm submachine gun, cheaply manufactured in the rush to compensate for weapons lost at Dunkirk. The Sten Mk I weighed 8.16 pounds, featuring a crude wooden foregrip and a 32-round box magazine, extending horizontally from the left side of the receiver. British factories produced 100,000 Stens in a matter of months, and the process was further streamlined with introduction of the Mk II in 1941, eliminating the forward pistol grip. Both models featured a tubular stock and fired at a cyclic rate of 550 rounds per minute.

Soviet submachine guns relied more heavily on wooden "furniture," but they were also mass produced with speed and economy in mind. The original PPD series weapons were chambered in 9mm, firing at a cyclic rate of 800 rounds per minute from 25-round box magazines or 71-round drums. A lighter weapon (11.9 pounds versus 12.54) was produced in the PPSh-41, chambered for 7.62mm, firing at a rate of 900 rounds per minute, using 35-round box magazines or 71-round drums.

As time went by and war in the Pacific merged with conflict in Korea, U.S. troops continued fighting with the weapons used in World War II, including the M1 Garand and M1 carbine, Browning machine guns, Thompson SMGs, the Colt .45 "automatic," and various shotguns. Surplus weapons from the last world war were also used by South Korean allies and the various United Nations forces that participated in the bloody "police action." Many new experiments were under way, but their results would not see light — or action — by the time a cease-fire was declared at Panmunjom.

Vietnam and Beyond

In World War II, technology had taken a long stride toward development of an all-purpose assault rifle, combining the functions of a traditional rifle with those of a light machine gun, but perfection remained elusive. Another step was taken by American inventors with production of the M14 in 1957. It had come too late to help with the Korean war, but in a few short years the weapon would be called upon to serve against another Asian enemy, in Vietnam.

The M14 was basically a modified M1 Garand, fitted out with a 20-round box magazine and a selective fire mechanism, permitting the shooter to choose between semiautomatic and fully automatic modes of operation. In practice, troops discovered that selective fire was rarely practical, since long bursts wasted ammunition and resulted in an overheated barrel. Chambered for the 7.62mm NATO round, weighing in at 8.55 pounds, many of the weapons were converted back to simple semiautomatic before their issuance to troops. In all, 1,380,346 M14s were manufactured before production ceased in 1964.

A new, experimental concept from the mind of arms designer Eugene Stoner was the Stoner 63 System, comprising seventeen modular units that could be arranged and assembled to create a whole panoply of weapons. Common components included the receiver, bolt and piston, the return spring, and the trigger mechanism, which were shared by all the different firearms. Other parts included butts and feed devices, different barrels, bi- and tripods. Employing drums and belts and magazines, the Stoner system could produce assault rifles, submachine guns, light machine guns, and so forth. Chambered in 5.56mm, the various arms maintained a consistent cyclic fire rate of 660 rounds per minute, the small projectiles compensating for their size by "tumbling" on impact with a target and producing massive wounds. Despite some use by Navy SEALs in Vietnam, the Stoner system, bogged down in its ambitious attempt to be all things to all men, never caught on.

Another weapon of Stoner's design, the M16 assault rifle, was officially adopted by the U.S. Army during 1961 as a replacement for the M14. Experience with fouling in the Asian jungles led to modification of the rifle's bolt closure device, with the revised M16A1 emerging in 1966. Used throughout the war in Vietnam and the invasion of Grenada, it remains the standard rifle issued to American military personnel. Capable of selective fire, the M16 and its shorter carbine version, the CAR-15, are chambered in 5.56mm, achieving a cyclic rate of 700 to 950 rounds per minute in full-auto mode. Attachment of a 40mm grenade launcher beneath the M16's barrel permits a rifleman to fire small, spin-stabilized grenades over a distance of 350 meters.

Shotguns played an active role in Vietnam, as in America's other wars of the late nineteenth and twentieth centuries. One popular model was the Ithaca 37, a 12-gauge weapon that loads and ejects rounds through the same port, on the underside of the receiver. (This arrangement makes the weapon truly ambidextrous, while sparing soldiers on the gunner's right from a barrage of smoking shells.) Experience in jungle warfare has singled out No. 4 shot as the optimum combat load, providing a balance of spread and penetration in thick undergrowth. The addition of specially designed "duckbill" chokes likewise encourages shot to spread laterally rather than vertically, increasing a lone gunner's potential kill ratio.

That grandfather of heavy machine guns, the Browning .50-caliber, saw extensive service in Vietnam as the modified M2 HB (heavy barrel). Ideal for use in fortified positions such as forward base camps, the guns were also mounted on armored personnel carriers for excursions into the hostile countryside.

America's light machine gun in Vietnam and Grenada was the M60, traceable to roots in the German designs of World War II. Chambered in 7.62mm, with a cyclic rate of 550 rounds per minute, the weapon was first issued in limited quantities during the late 1950s. Designed for squad support, the M60 is normally served by a three-man crew under combat conditions. Members of the team include the gunner (who carries the weapon); his "number two" (packing three boxes of ammunition, spare parts, and a cleaning kit); and his "number three" (bearing more ammo, along with the 6.7-pound tripod). Other members of the rifle squad were often forced to carry surplus ammunition for the '60, in addition to their own equipment, leading to its nickname, "the pig." Variant forms include the M60C (remote-fired for external mounting on helicopters), the M60D (pintle-mounted, minus buttstock, in helicopters), and the M60E2 (a much-altered coaxial gun, mounted in armored vehicles).

We've come a long way from the slopes of San Juan Hill and belching muskets, but the basic job of combat soldiers still remains the same: to kill the enemy in numbers that will force him to retreat or raise a flag of truce. Of course, the enemy has similar intentions, and it's time for us to make a survey of the hardware that's been pointing our way from the other side of no-man's land.

BEHIND ENEMY LINES

As seen in Chapter 4, the U.S. Ordnance Board was slow to yield to nineteenth-century firearm innovations like the jacketed bullet and smokeless gunpowder. Another golden opportunity was missed with the introduction of the Mauser bolt-action rifle in 1868, and American soldiers would pay for that mistake with their lives thirty years later in the war with Spain.

Peter Paul Mauser was a mechanical genius, almost single-handedly responsible for designing the first successful metallic-cartridge bolt-action rifles. His revolutionary designs included automatic cam cocking, the principles of bolt-head design, elastic extractors, primary extraction, ejectors, a manual safety device, and an improved locking lug system — in short, every desirable feature of the metallic-cartridge bolt-action rifle. Countless modern weapons still rely upon the Mauser innovations for their strength, and it is fair to say that Mauser stands beside the likes of Maxim, Colt, and Browning in the firearms hall of fame.

Ironically, the young inventor's native Germany showed little interest in his first designs, and he was forced to go abroad — as Browning left America for Europe — to secure backing for a prototype. Mauser's first patent was obtained in 1868 in the United States, but military eyes were blind to previews of the future. When the Ordnance Board started shopping for magazine rifles in 1890, they bypassed excellent Mausers in favor of the Krag-Jorgensen model. Our potential enemies, meanwhile, were buying Mauser arms as fast as they could come off the assembly line.

The Spanish-American War

Spain adopted its first Mauser rifle in 1891, seven years before the outbreak of hostilities with the United States. Chambered in 7.62mm with smokeless cartridges, the weapons were produced in both rifle and carbine versions, with their in-line magazines protruding below the stock. The 1892 Mauser introduced a new 7mm cartridge and a nonrotating extractor attached to the bolt by a collar. The latest cartridge generated a muzzle velocity of 2,650 feet per second.

Spain's most famous Mauser was the 7mm Model 1893, which introduced the integral staggered-row box magazine, holding five rounds. It measured 48.6 inches overall (or 41.3 inches in the short version) and weighed in at 8.8 pounds (8.3 for the shorty). Both weapons were sturdy and accurate, incorporating a simplified safety lock and an improved bolt stop.

Along with the Model 1895 Mauser carbine, these were the weapons which pinned American riflemen down at El Caney, inflicting casualties of 10 percent on U.S. troops at San Juan Hill. Captured by the thousands between 1896 and 1898, Mausers were subjected to intensive scrutiny in Washington, and when the famous "Springfield" rifle surfaced five years later, it would use the Mauser '93's extractor system basically unchanged. If nothing else, America was slowly learning from her own mistakes.

World War I

When German soldiers went to war in 1914, they were armed with the rugged Mauser rifle designated as Gewehr 1898. Measuring 49.2 inches overall, the piece weighed 9.26 pounds and fed its

7.92mm cartridges from a five-round integral box magazine. The pointed "spitzer" bullets had a muzzle velocity of 2,100 feet per second, but their most unusual quality was discovered by pure chance. In 1916, after British troops introduced the first tanks, marksmen somehow discovered that Mauser rounds, fired "backwards," had the capability of piercing armor plate. If loaded with the blunt end foremost, they would punch through steel before the bullet had a chance to warp and lose velocity in flight. Thus, by accident, the Mauser '98 established itself as both an excellent combat rifle and the first antitank weapon!

Pistols played a major role in trench warfare, and German troops had no shortage of models to choose from. Adopted in 1908 as the standard military side arm, the 9mm Pistole '08 is more commonly recognized by the name of its designer, Georg Luger. Weighing 1.93 pounds, the Luger carried an eight-round magazine in its butt, and the 9mm Parabellum ("for war") rounds sizzled down range at a muzzle velocity of 1,050 feet per second. Different models were produced with barrels ranging from 4 to 12 inches in length, the latter mounted on an Artillery Model that also sported a combination wooden shoulder stock and holster, plus a 32-round "snail" drum.

The classic Luger was a work of art, and it became a cherished souvenir for U.S. troops in both world wars. The rake of the butt made comfortable shooting, but the weapon's most distinctive feature was the upward-opening toggle mechanism mounted atop the receiver. In action, the toggle was opened by recoil action, ejecting the spent round and chambering another as a spring in the butt reset the mechanism in its starting position. Consisting almost entirely of handmade parts, the Luger was relatively difficult to manufacture, and the vital toggle mechanism quickly fouled upon exposure to the muddy trenches.

The eruption of hostilities produced an overnight demand for pistols that the costly, complicated Luger could not hope to meet. In answer to the crisis, German soldiers dusted off the Modell 1879 revolver, a low-powered weapon chambered in 10.6mm (.417 caliber). The '79's rounds never exceeded a muzzle velocity of 673 feet per second, and they were soon supplanted by a pair of mass-produced semiautomatic pistols, dubbed the Dreyse and Langenham. Chambered for 9mm Parabellum and 7.65mm respectively, both weapons were simpler (and cheaper) than the classic Luger, but neither would ever succeed in replacing the Pistole '08 as Germany's standard-issue side arm.

Another handgun carried to the front in World War I was the Mauser C/96, dubbed the "broom handle" after its distinctive wooden butt. Weighing in at 2.69 pounds, chambered in either 7.63mm or 9mm, the Mauser was introduced as a cavalry weapon in 1896, its hammer designed to be cocked on a horseman's thigh. The ten-round magazine lay forward of the trigger-guard, and was loaded from above with a metal clip, in a style later emulated by the American Garand rifle. A semiautomatic weapon as designed originally, Mauser's pistol has been emulated far and wide by other nations. (Recently, the Red Chinese began producing full-automatic copies for export to revolutionary "freedom fighters" around the world.)

The German army was slow to accept Hiram Maxim's machine gun designs, but one model — the MG 08, dubbed the "Spandau" — had been adopted by 1908. A true heavy machine gun at 136.7 pounds, the Spandau was water cooled and chambered in 7.92mm, firing at a cyclic rate of 300 to 450 rounds per minute. Its ponderous sledge mount, weighing another 83 pounds, was designed to fold up, with the Spandau on top, permitting the gun to be dragged across country from one battlefront to the next. In practice, the Spandau was normally emplaced in sturdy dugouts, surrounded by sand bags and thickets of barbed wire, from which it claimed a fearful toll of Allied lives.

A modified version of the Spandau, designated as the MG 08/15, tried for greater mobility with a reduced water jacket plus an added shoulder stock and pistol grip. Worlds lighter than the original, at 39.7 pounds, the MG 08/15 still failed to qualify as a true light machine gun, but at least it was portable. The original Spandau's firing mechanism was retained, achieving a cyclic rate of 450 rounds per minute, and a variant air-cooled form — the LMG 08/15 — was designed for use on aircraft, fired by means of a cable, and synchronized with the individual plane's propeller.

Near the end of the war, German inventors broke new ground with their introduction of the first practical submachine gun, dubbed the Maschinenpistole 18. Chambered for the 9mm Parabellum pistol cartridge, utilizing the blowback principle of operation

[Chapter 4], the MP 18 was a revolutionary design, but its late arrival at the front prevented it from having a decisive impact on the outcome of the war.

Austro-Hungarian riflemen carried the bolt-action Mannlicher Modell 1895 when they marched off to battle in 1914. Chambered in 8mm, the weapon used a five-round box magazine and weighed in at 8.3 pounds, fully loaded. At 50 inches overall, the Mannlicher was uncomfortably long for trench fighting, but a shorter carbine version was introduced during the first year of combat.

The standard Austro-Hungarian Empire side arm in World War I was the Steyer-Hahn M.12 semiautomatic pistol, chambered in 9mm. With a full eight-round magazine in place, it weighed 2.25 pounds, achieving a muzzle velocity of 1,115 feet per second. As always, the demands of war outpaced production, and imperial troops were frequently armed with alternative handguns. One such weapon was the M.1898, a sturdy revolver issued to officers and NCOs during the late nineteenth and early twentieth centuries. Chambered in 8mm, the piece was unusual both for its cartridge and its unique mode of field stripping, in which a downward tug on the trigger guard exposed the internal works for cleaning or repair.

Austro-Hungarian forces adopted their first semiautomatic pistol nine years later, designated the M.07. Another 8mm weapon, the M.07 carried its ten-round magazine in front of the triggerguard, Mauser-style, and employed a unique firing mechanism. On detonation of the cartridge, a long bolt moved backward with the barrel, continuing its motion once the barrel was halted by stops. A complex ejection-feed process climaxed when the bolt and barrel snapped back to their original position, powered by a return spring. Manufacturing complications finally doomed the design, and five years after its introduction the weapon was supplanted by the simpler M.12.

The empire's first indigenous machine gun was designed by Andreas Schwarzlose in 1902, leading to production of a series that included the Modell 07, Modell 08, and Modell 12. All were heavy belt-fed weapons, chambered in 8mm, with the Modell 12 weighing in at 43.87 pounds, mounted on a tripod of equal weight. The weapon achieved a cyclic fire rate of 400 rounds per minute, employing the "delayed blowback" system. In this format, the heavy breechblock is held in place by a levered mechanism, powered backward by recoil only *after* a bullet has flown from the barrel. The system's obvious drawback is barrel length, with relatively short barrels required to keep the gun from stalling, thereby shaving range and accuracy. The original Schwarzlose machine guns used special lubricated ammunition, but this feature was eliminated in the Modell 12, and older guns were revamped to meet the new weapon's standards after 1912.

Italy formed the Triple Alliance with Germany and Austria-Hungary in the 1880s, and while she later dropped out, switching sides to line up with the Allies in 1915, I've included her here for the sake of consistency. Authors of historical fiction will naturally wish to confirm crucial dates before launching Italian troops against one side or the other.

The standard weapon of Italian riflemen in World War I was the Fucile Modello 91, better known as the Mannlicher Carcano (of JFK assassination fame). Developed between 1890 and 1891, this piece was an amalgamation of the classic Mauser bolt-action, a six-round box magazine of Mannlicher design, and a bolt-sleeve safety device invented by Salvatore Carcano. Chambered in 6.5mm, the rifle measured 50.6 inches overall and weighed 8.4 pounds. Adopted for military service in 1892, it remained the official Italian rifle until World War II. A shorter variant, the Moschetto Modello 91, was produced at the same time, designed as a cavalry carbine, complete with folding bayonet.

At the outbreak of war, Italian forces were armed with semi-automatic pistols designated as Modello 1910, chambered for the puny Glisenti 9mm cartridge, with a maximum muzzle velocity of 846 feet per second. The chamber would also accommodate 9mm Parabellum rounds, but this was a compromise measure at best, and the Glisentis were soon replaced with the superior Beretta Modello 1915. Available in 7.65mm or 9mm, the Berettas weighed 1.25 pounds with their eight-round magazine in place. Employing a simple blowback mechanism with concealed hammer, they lacked the stylistic finesse of later Berettas, but the 1915 was still a vast improvement over the feeble Glisentis.

Pistols held a special value for Italian troops in World War I, as teams of "Deathshead" pioneers went scuttling through the trenches, seeking out their enemies (whomever they might be) for combat hand-to-hand. Clad in helmets, mail, and upper-body armor reminiscent of medieval knights, the Deathshead troopers fought exclusively with pistols, knives, and their entrenching tools, which served as handy battle axes in a pinch.

Italian forces made their solitary contribution to the field of automatic weapons with production of the Villar-Perosa, a curious double-barreled gun with dual overhead magazines. Chambered for pistol ammunition, the Villar-Perosa is frequently hailed as the "first submachine gun," but it fails to qualify since none were ever carried into battle by the infantry. Instead, the guns were uniformly mounted in the style of light machine guns, to defend emplaced positions, and they never functioned in the submachine gun's classic role, as did the German MP 18.

Axis Arms of World War II

It is, perhaps, superfluous to note that Nazi Germany was overrun with oddballs — racist "supermen," raving homosexuals, "mad scientists" obsessed with twins, and weird occultists struggling to prove their theory of a hollow earth — but there were also geniuses at large in the asylum. (After World War II, German rocket scientists were variously hired or kidnapped by Americans and Soviets alike, their work with jets and guided missiles paving the way to the Space Age.) In arms development, German inventors took the common foot soldier from bolt-action arms to full-auto assault rifles in the space of five short years, and modern war has never been the same.

Germany's standard rifle at the onset of World War II was the same Gewehr 98 that the Kaiser's troops had used in the conflict of 1914-18. A modified version, the Karabiner 98k (for *kurz*, or "short") was also chambered in 7.92mm, featuring accessories that included grenade launchers, periscopic sights, and a folding buttstock on the model issued to airborne troops. Shorter (43.6 inches) and lighter (8.6 pounds) than its ancestor, the '98 carbine also produced a greater muzzle velocity, hurling its bullets down range at an average rate of 2,477 feet per second.

"Lightning-war" created a demand for new equipment, and German designers responded with production of two modern rifles, the Gewehr 41 and Gewehr 43. Both were gas-operated weapons, chambered in 7.92mm with ten-round box magazines and an average muzzle velocity of 2,546 feet per second. The Gewehr 41 measured 44.25 inches overall and weighed in at 11.09 pounds, with a telescopic sight mounted as standard equipment. An excellent sniper rifle, it turned up mostly on the Eastern front, in use against the Soviets. A quarter-inch shorter, and lighter (at 9.7 pounds), the Gewehr 43 evolved from the study of captured Tokarev weapons, using the Soviet mechanism virtually unchanged. Popular with front-line troops for its easy loading and rapid rate of semiautomatic fire, the piece was modified as the Karabiner 43, introduced in 1944, to include manufacture with wood laminates and plastics.

Ever jealous of the army, Goering's Luftwaffe struggled to produce its own self-loading rifle through the early 1940s. The result was a complex gas-operated weapon, designated the FG 42, which saw its first operational use in Skorzeny's daring commando raid to rescue Mussolini from house arrest. Chambered in 7.92mm, the weapon measured 37 inches overall, tipped the scales at 9.99 pounds, and sported a side-mounted 20-round box magazine. Resembling a light machine gun in outline, it sprayed full-automatic fire at cyclic rate of 750 to 800 rounds per minute, achieving a muzzle velocity of 2,500 feet per second. For all that, the FG 42 was costly and difficult to manufacture, still suffering from many "bugs" when V-E day put an end to production.

Germany's leap into the field of assault rifle development came with production of the Maschinenkarabiner 42, a 7.92mm weapon designed by Louis Schmeisser during 1940-41. A batch of the experimental arms were air-dropped to a paratroop battalion on the Eastern front, surrounded by the Soviets, and enthusiasm ran high after the troops fought their way clear. Hitler, in his wisdom, instantly demanded that production cease, but members of his staff ignored the order, forging ahead with development under a new designation, as Maschinenpistole 43.

Reversals on the Eastern front made firepower a top priority, and the new MP 43s turned up first in the hands of elite fighting units. (A variant form, the MP 43/1, was produced with fittings for a grenade-launching cup on its muzzle.) Rescinding his prior opposition in 1944, Hitler renamed this weapon the StG 44, and production continued with few, if any, alterations. The finished product measured 37 inches overall and weighed 11.5 pounds with its 30-round box magazine, achieving a cyclic fire rate of 500 rounds per minute. Accessories included a red night-fighter scope called the *Vampir*, and a curved barrel with periscopic mirror sights, designed for firing around corners!

Countless Luger P 08s remained in circulation at the outbreak of the war, but they were slated for replacement by the Walther P38, a 9mm side arm first issued to Panzer troops in 1938. Tipping the scales at 2.12 pounds with a loaded eight-round magazine, the Walther was — and is — an excellent service pistol, valued for both comfort and accuracy by troopers who received them before war's end. Many officers clung to their traditional Lugers — and the stylish guns remained a favored souvenir with Yanks in France — but conventional "automatics" were clearly the wave of the future.

Two more offerings from Walther were the PP (Polizei Pistole) and PPK ("k" for *kurz* or "short") models. First manufactured as a police side arm in 1929, the Walther PP weighed 1.5 pounds with its eight-round magazine in place. Its lighter cousin (by a quarter-pound) held seven rounds and was designed for easier concealment during plain-clothes work. Available in calibers ranging from .22 to 9mm, the light Walthers continued in service with German police officers and Gestapo agents, with some turning up in the hands of Luftwaffe air crews.

The Versailles Treaty of 1919 had specifically banned development of new machine guns in Germany, but research continued in Switzerland, under cover of various "shadow" companies. The resultant product was a weapon called the Rheinmetall MG 15, chambered in 7.92mm, which long remained in production for use by the Luftwaffe. More important, the Rheinmetall design also evolved into a separate and distinct piece, designated the MG 34, still regarded as one of the finest machine guns produced in the twentieth century.

Like its ancestor, the MG 34 was chambered for 7.92mm, measuring 48 inches overall and tipping the scales at 25.4 pounds with its bipod attached. Also capable of mounting on a tripod, the weapon fired at a cyclic rate of 800 to 900 rounds per minute, feeding ammunition from 50-round belts or distinctive 75-round saddle drums. Variant models included the MG 34m (with a heavier barrel jacket, for use in armored vehicles), the MG 34s (a shorter version), and the MG 34/41 (designed for antiaircraft deployment).

In time, the MG 34's own excellence became a drawback, making reproduction of the weapon slow and costly. Searching for a cheaper, "easy" weapon as the war progressed, the Germans studied various designs captured in Poland and Czechoslovakia, and produced another first-class machine gun in the form of their MG 42. As the first machine gun manufactured via mass production, the MG 42 utilized numerous metal stampings in place of handmade parts, but quality and performance somehow survived the shift. Chambered in 7.92mm, the weapon's dimensions and weight were identical with the MG 34, but it boasted a prodigious rate of fire, inhaling ammunition at a cyclic rate of 1,550 rounds per minute. Introduced during 1942 in both the Soviet Union and North Africa, the MG 42 produced a sound like heavy canvas ripping as it went to work. Incredibly, a later variant, the MG 45, possessed an even higher rate of fire.

Pioneers in the field of submachine gun development, the Germans dusted off their MP 18s ten years later, revamping them with new sights and minor internal adjustments to produce the MP 28. A 9mm weapon, the new model weighed in at 11.56 pounds and measured 32.09 inches overall. Its various magazines — 20- or 30-round box and a 32-round "snail" drum — were mounted on the left side of the weapon, feeding ammunition through the chamber at a cyclic rate of 350 to 450 rounds per minute.

Germany's next development, the MP 35, resembled the '28 at first glance, but its magazine port had been shifted to the right side, the bolt rear-mounted to cut down on fouling in combat. The modified trigger utilized a double-pressure system, with light contact producing single shots and full pressure producing sustained automatic fire. Chambered in 9mm, the MP 35 measured 33.07 inches overall and weighed 10.43 pounds. It also improved on the MP 28's rate of fire, averaging 650 rounds per minute from 24- or 32-round magazines. As it turned out, the weapon was extremely popular with members of the Waffen SS, and Hitler's elite unit purchased all existing pieces after late 1940.

The Reich's most famous submachine gun was the MP 38, immortalized in Yankee parlance as the "Schmeisser." (Ironically, inventor Hugo Schmeisser had nothing to do with the weapon's design or production; its G.I. christening remains a total mystery.) Following the earlier example of the MG 42, this weapon revolutionized small-arms design by relying entirely on simple metal stampings, die-cast parts, and substitution of plastic for the traditional wooden "furniture." Fitted with a folding wire butt, the MP 38 featured a sheet metal body and minimal machining on the breechblock. A 9mm weapon operating on the blow back principle, it measured 32.8 inches overall, weighed 10.36 pounds, and sported a 32-round vertical box magazine. Its cyclic fire rate of 500 rounds per minute was a compromise between earlier models, conserving ammunition while still providing foot soldiers with impressive firepower.

In practice, the "Schmeisser" fired from an open breech, and by 1939 a built-in problem had revealed itself to front-line troops. Simply stated, when the gun was cocked, a simple jolt could make it fire without a finger on the trigger, spewing lethal rounds of "friendly fire." The answer was arrived at with addition of a pin, designed to lock the breechblock open when the gun was cocked but not in use. The revised model was designated as the MG 38/40, with a cheaper, simpler MP 40 version manufactured as the war went on.

Italian troops in World War II were armed with a bizarre collection of the poorest rifles used by any of the primary combatants. Dusting off their stock from World War I, suppliers met demands initially with thousands of the Mannlicher Carcano M1891 and its shorter carbine version (discussed under World War I, earlier). A later, equally inferior production was the Mannlicher Carcano M1938, available in either 6.5mm or 7.35mm, using the traditional Mannlicher six-round box magazine. Measuring 40.2 inches overall, it tipped the scales at 7.5 pounds, while the carbine version weighed in a pound lighter and four inches shorter. Italy's most modern rifle was the 6.5mm Mannlicher Carcano M1941, another cheap bolt-action, but its appearance was balanced by the wartime resurrection of numerous 8mm Mannlichers from 1889 and 1895, with a number of decrepit Vetterli Vitali rifles lately rebarreled for 6.5mm rounds.

In contrast to their miserable shoulder arms, the Italians produced an excellent pistol in the Beretta Modello 1934. Chambered in 9mm Short (.380 automatic), the gun measured six inches overall and weighed 1.25 pounds with its seven-round magazine in place. Unlike the Modello 1915, this weapon featured an exposed hammer, and its muzzle velocity of 950 feet per second compared favorably with the Colt .45's 825 fps. As with the American Colt, the Beretta's receiver locked open after the last shot was fired from its magazine, but *un*like other pistols featuring this mechanism, the receiver snapped forward again as soon as the empty magazine was removed. (The Colt's — and those of later Berettas — remain open to facilitate swift reloading.)

Italy's standard machine gun was the Breda Modello 30, a weapon of odd appearance and barely adequate performance. Chambered in 6.5mm, the gun measured 48.5 inches overall and weighed 22.75 pounds, feeding ammunition (when it functioned) from 20-round chargers at a cyclic rate of 450 to 500 rounds per minute. The inferior extraction system demanded an interior oil pump to lubricate spent casings, and the oil in turn attracted grime, resulting in numerous failures. Another design glitch, omission of carrying handles, required Italian gunners to wear heavy gloves when they handled the weapon in combat.

The Breda Modello 31 was Italy's heavy machine gun, chambered in .50 caliber and designed for use on armored vehicles. Again, design was faulty, and the weapon's large, curved overhead magazine made it virtually useless in tight places — like the inside of a tank. Designers tried to give the infantry a break with the new Breda Modello 37, and while the weapon was a slight improvement over the '31, it still retained its ancestor's troublesome oil-lubricating mechanism. Further, it employed a flat 20-round feed tray that worked its way through the receiver as rounds were expended, catching spent shells. In practice, this meant that gunners had to dump the useless casings out before they could reload the tray, creating one more problem for a soldier under fire. For all its problems, the 8mm Modello 37 became Italy's standard heavy machine gun, measuring 50 inches overall and weighing 42.8 pounds, with a 41.2-pound tripod. When the mechanism functioned, it achieved a cyclic rate of 450 to 500 rounds per minute.

Once more, in contrast to the general poor condition of Italian automatic weapons, the Beretta Model 1938A submachine gun was a standout, recognized for excellence, with no expense spared in its production. Notable for its distinctive double triggers, the

Beretta was chambered in 9mm and measured 37.24 inches overall, tipping the scales at 10.96 pounds. Its average cyclic rate of fire was 600 rounds per minute, using 10-, 20-, 30-, and 40-round box magazines, all of which were issued with convenient loading devices. Regarded by collectors as a work of art, the World War II Beretta ranks among the most accurate submachine guns ever produced.

Adopted in 1905, the Japanese Rifle Type 38 combined Mauser and Mannlicher design points with a few indigenous innovations. Chambered in 6.5mm, the weapon's small caliber and special low-powered cartridge produced a light recoil preferred by diminutive Japanese soldiers. Conversely, the weapon's 50-inch overall length, increased with the attachment of a fearsome bayonet, extended a small man's reach for hand-to-hand combat. A shorter version, the Carbine Type 38, was also produced (including a folding-butt model for airborne troops), while the Sniper's Rifle Type 97 featured a revised bolt handle and provision for a telescopic sight.

A new weapon, designated as Rifle Type 99, was basically the old Type 38 revised to chamber 7.7mm (.303 caliber) ammunition. Early production models featured a folding monopod, for greater accuracy, and new sights designed for sniping at low-flying aircraft, but the rigors of war damaged production standards, and most of the frills were discarded after Pearl Harbor.

Japan's standard military side arm through the early 1930s was the "Nambu," designated Pistol Type 14. Chambered in 8mm, the weapon's production could never keep pace with demand after Japan's full-scale invasion of China, and military procurers began shopping around for replacements. Their eventual choice, Pistol Type 94, had entered commercial production in 1934 and was soon co-opted by the army. One of the worst service pistols in history, Type 94 was ugly, poorly designed, and difficult to handle. Feeding the puny 8mm Taisho 14 cartridge from a six-round box magazine, this shoddy piece was capable of accidentally discharging rounds before they had been fully seated in the firing chamber!

Japanese heavy machine guns in World War II were all derived from the Hotchkiss mechanism with minimal changes, but designers were more innovative in the field of light machine guns. An early model, Light Machine Gun Type 11, remained in service from 1922 through 1945, serving troops on the Asian mainland and across the Pacific. Evolved from the Hotchkiss design, with internal revisions by Gen. Kijiro Nambu, the Type 11 was chambered in 6.5mm, measured 43.5 inches overall, and weighed 22.5 pounds. Firing at a cyclic rate of 500 rounds per minute, the weapon was served by a 30-round hopper mounted to the left of the receiver, intended for use with the standard military rifle cartridge. In practice, rifle rounds were too powerful for the gun's delicate internal mechanism, and special low-powered rounds were required for successful operation. Even so, the hopper's placement left the Type 11 poorly balanced, and its use of the Italian-style oil-lubrication system created persistent problems with fouling.

A variation of the Type 11, dubbed the Tank Machine Gun Type 91, was basically the same weapon, fitted out with a 50-round hopper, and no real improvement was seen until production of the Light Machine Gun Type 96, in 1936. Chambered in 6.5mm, the new weapon measured 41.5 inches and weighed 20 pounds, devouring 30-round overhead box magazines at a cyclic fire rate of 550 rounds per minute. While incorporating features from the Czech ZB vz 26, encountered by Japanese troops in China, the Type 96 retained the ill-conceived oil pump and suffered accordingly.

The Japanese were slow in development of an indigenous submachine gun, producing their Type 100 in 1942. Chambered in 8mm, the weapon (and its subsequent revised models) measured 35.43 inches overall and weighed 9.7 pounds, mounting a curved box magazine on the left side of the receiver. The original cyclic fire rate of 450 rounds per minute had been improved to 800 rpm by the appearance of a third and final variant, in 1944, but overall production declined through the years, with the sights reduced to crude aiming posts in later versions. Victimized by the demand for mass-production, soldiers armed with later Type 100s would find themselves at a distinct disadvantage when accuracy was required.

Communist Arms of The Korean War

As a client state of the Soviet Union, North Korea received large shipments of surplus arms and ammunition in the postwar era. Manufacturing was rudimentary at best in the "People's Republic," and so the troops of Kim Il Sun depended on Stalin's largesse to maintain the revolutionary war machine. When the North Koreans pushed off across the 38th Parallel in June 1950, Russian T-34 tanks led the way, backed by infantry packing a wide range of Soviet arms.

Most North Korean riflemen were issued the M1891/30 rifle, chambered in 7.62mm, which the Soviets first manufactured during 1930. Measuring 48.5 inches overall, minus a 17-inch bayonet, the weapon weighed in at 9.7 pounds with bayonet and sling attached. A bolt-action piece with a five-round box magazine, the M1891/30 was also available in a sniper version, tipping the scales at 11.3 pounds with its telescopic sight.

A secondary weapon issued to North Korean troops was the Soviet M1944 carbine, chambered in 7.62mm. The last of the Mosin-Nagant designs, it boasted a permanently fixed bayonet and weighed 8.9 pounds, measuring 40 inches with bayonet folded, versus 52.25 inches with the blade extended. Another bolt-action piece with five-round magazine, the M1944 generated a lower muzzle velocity (at 2,514 feet per second) than the older M1891/30 (at 2,660 fps).

Without a service pistol of their own, North Koreans packed the Soviet Tokarev TT-33 on their long march south. At the other end of the scale, they were also armed with the Russian 12mm (.50-caliber) DShK M1938 heavy machine gun. Both weapons were covered in Chapter 4, and I'll spare the reader needless repetition here.

An older machine gun, the PM1910, was also on hand when the reds launched their invasion of South Korea. A standard Maxim weapon, chambered in 7.62mm, the PM1910 had been Russia's main weapon in World War I, remaining in continuous production from 1910 through 1943. Water-cooled and belt-fed, with a cyclic rate of 520 to 600 rounds per minute, the weapon and tripod weighed 163 pounds, requiring at least two men to drag the assembly from one point to another in combat.

In the realm of light machine guns, North Korea used the Soviet DP and DPM models, chambered in 7.62mm. Air-cooled weapons using identical overhead drum magazines, both models measured 50 inches overall, but the DP was marginally lighter (at 26.23 pounds) than the DPM (at 26.9 pounds). As the war progressed, Korean factories produced their own 7.62mm copies of the Soviet PPSh M1941 submachine gun, already covered in Chapter 4.

Another late addition to the communist orbit, Red China was also dependent on Soviet arms. Unlike North Korea, the Chinese soon tooled up for full-scale production of copies, each christened in turn with a new, "original" designation. Thus, when Chinese soldiers crossed the Yalu River to confront Americans in October 1950, they carried the Type 53 Rifle (the Mosin-Nagant M1944 carbine, discussed earlier), the Type 51 Pistol (Russia's Tokarev TT-33), the Type 53 Light Machine Gun (the Soviet DPM), and the Type 50 Submachine Gun (Russia's PPSh M1941). [See Chapter 4 for details on the Russian arms of World War II.]

Enemy Weapons in Vietnam

The eviction of French colonial troops in 1954 initially left the victorious Viet Minh communists with large stocks of captured arms and ammunition on hand. Subsequent partition of Indochina into North and South Vietnam brought Soviet and Chinese support for the northern regime of Ho Chi Minh, with substantial infusions of Russian arms and their Red Chinese look-alikes. Later, when Viet Cong guerrillas launched their subversive campaign in the south, they fought primarily with weapons from North Vietnam, picking up captured American arms where they could.

The North Vietnamese Army (NVA) and the Viet Cong were originally armed with Soviet Mosin-Nagant M1944 carbines or their Chinese Type 53 equivalents. The introduction of American personnel after 1954 led to capture and theft of M1 carbines, M14s, and later M16s. In time, the standard arm of both the NVA and Viet Cong would be the outstanding Soviet AK-47 assault rifle and AKS carbine, or the Chinese carbon-copy Type 56 Assault Rifle and Type 56 Carbine. These weapons are covered later, in the section dealing with Warsaw Pact weapons.

NVA regulars and the VC normally carried the Tokarev TT-33 pistol or its Chinese Type 51 equivalent, but quantities of the U.S. .45-caliber M1911A1 Colt were also captured over time. In addition to stock on hand, North Vietnamese factories were equipped to produce copies of both the American Colt .45 and the high-powered Browning 9mm pistol.

While generally supplying VC forces with their military needs across the board, North Vietnamese troops kept the heavy Soviet ZPU4 machine guns to themselves. Useless in fluid conditions of guerrilla warfare, the ZPU4 consists of a four-wheeled mount with four KPV heavy machine guns arranged together for mass firing. The guns are chambered in 14.5mm, measuring 78.7 inches overall and firing at a cyclic rate of 600 rounds per minute. A powerful antiaircraft weapon, the ZPU4 was supplemented in North Vietnam by captured Browning .50-caliber M2 HBs, mounted on Soviet DShK carriages with Soviet sights attached for use against low-flying jets.

Other heavy machine guns, used by VC and NVA regulars alike, included the 12.7mm DShK M1938 (or Chinese Type 54 Heavy Machine Gun), the 7.62mm SG 43 (or Chinese Type 53), and the 7.62mm SGM (or Chinese Type 57). All of these arms are covered in Chapter 4, in the section dealing with Soviet weapons of World War II.

Light machine guns shared by the Viet Cong and North Vietnamese included American M60s captured in combat, Soviet DPMs or their Chinese Type 53 equivalents [covered in Chapter 4], and the Soviet RPD model [of which we'll say more in a moment]. Rounding off the list of options were the Soviet RP 46 and its Chinese carbon copy, the Type 58 Light Machine Gun. Chambered in 7.62mm, this weapon measured 40.9 inches overall and fired at a cyclic rate of 600 rounds per minute, feeding ammunition from a 40-round box magazine or a 75-round drum. Its design was basically the same as the Degtyarev guns discussed in Chapter 4.

Starting with a motley collection of Thompsons and French 9mm Model 49 submachine guns—the latter rebarreled for 7.62mm when stocks of captured ammunition ran low—NVA regulars and their Viet Cong allies later obtained Soviet PPS M1943 and PPSh M1941 submachine guns in substantial quantities. The Chinese version of the PPSh M1941—designated as the Type 50 Submachine Gun—was a blowback-operated weapon with selective fire capabilities and a telescopic wire butt, consuming 35-round box magazines at a cyclic rate of 900 rounds per minute.

The Warsaw Pact

Organized in 1955 to counter NATO, the Warsaw Pact consists of the USSR and its client states in Albania, Bulgaria, Czechoslovakia, Hungary, Poland, Rumania, and East Germany. Unlike NATO, in which all members have a voice in shaping policy, the

Soviets clearly speak for their Eastern European "allies" — and, with a single exception discussed later, they also provide the bulk of military weapons used in communist nations.

Chief among those weapons is the AK-47 assault rifle, designed by Mikhail Kalashnikov. (Please note the spelling, here. Despite innumerable published blunders, there is no such weapon as the "Klashnikov," "Kalishnakov," or any of a dozen other clumsy variations.) Introduced as an experimental piece in 1946, the standard model entered service during 1957 and is generally acknowledged as the finest weapon of its type to date. Chambered in 7.62mm, the AK-47 with fixed wooden butt measures 34.21 inches (a folding metal stock is also available) and weighs 11.31 pounds with a loaded 30-round box magazine. Evolved from the German assault rifles of World War II, the Kalashnikov is also manufactured in Poland, East Germany, and China — where, as the Type 56 Assault Rifle, it comes with an integral folding bayonet. Firing at a cyclic rate of 300 to 400 rounds per minute, the AK-47 makes a distinctive sound seldom forgotten by soldiers on the receiving end.

Variants of the original Kalashnikov include the AKM (with a muzzle brake and simpler internal design), the AKMS (with a folding steel butt), and the AKM-63 (manufactured in Hungary). Soviet forces are now in the process of replacing their old-line Kalashnikovs with the new AK-74, chambered in 5.45mm, but the "obsolete" weapons remain in action throughout the Eastern Bloc and Asia, turning up in the hands of irregular forces including the PLO and Al Fatah, the Irish Republican Army, and the African National Congress. Perhaps the most prolific weapon in the world, the AK-47 and its variants have proven their ability to function smoothly from the Asian jungles to the desert wasteland of the Middle East.

A maverick weapon manufactured in Czechoslovakia, the Vz.58 bears a strong external resemblance to the Kalashnikov, but its trigger assembly and locking mechanism are radically different. Chambered in 7.62mm, the rifle measures 32.28 inches overall and weighs 8.24 pounds with its 30-round box magazine. In spite of the mechanical revisions — or perhaps because of them — the Vz.58 roughly doubles the Kalashnikov's rate of fire, averaging 800 rounds per minute in full-auto mode.

One last addition to the rifle category is the SVD "Dragunov," a Soviet sniper rifle introduced in 1963. Chambered in 7.62mm, this gas-operated semiautomatic weapon measures 48.23 inches overall and packs a ten-round magazine, hurling projectiles down range at a muzzle velocity of 2,723 feet per second. In its standard configuration, the SVD mounts an excellent PSO-1 telescopic sight, featuring a graduated range-finding scale.

The venerable Tokarev pistol has been replaced in Warsaw Pact nations by the Soviet Makarov PM, a 9mm weapon developed in the late 1950s. Measuring 6.3 inches overall, the piece weighs 1.46 pounds without its eight-round magazine. Essentially a blown-up version of the Walther PP side arm [Chapter 4], the Makarov uses a simple blowback system, feeding new cartridges of intermediate power, between the 9mm Short and the more powerful 9mm Parabellum. Known as Pistole M in East Germany and Type 59 in Red China, the weapon is also manufactured in Poland as the P-64.

Warsaw Pact machine guns run the gamut of the Russian PK series, introduced in 1946 and slightly modified in later years. The basic weapon is chambered in 7.62mm, belt-fed at a cyclic rate of 690 to 720 rounds per minute. It measures 45.67 inches overall and weighs 19.84 pounds, with the standard tripod adding another 16.53 pounds. Different models in the series include the PKS (tripod-mounted), the PKT (on armored vehicles), the PKM (with bipod), the PKMS (a tripod-mounted PKM), and the PKB (with spade bits and "butterfly" trigger, recalling the old Vickers guns). Striving for originality, the Red Chinese refer to their PK machine guns as Type 80.

A light machine gun used for squad support, the Soviet RPK is actually an enlarged version of the AKM assault rifle, introduced in 1966. Christened Type 74 by the Chinese, Russia's RPK is chambered in 7.62mm, firing at a cyclic rate of 660 rounds per minute from 30- or 40-round box magazines, with an alternate 75-round drum. The piece measures 40.75 inches overall, and weighs 15.65 pounds. A modified version, the RPK-74, has been designed for use with the new Soviet 5.45mm cartridge.

The RPD machine gun, introduced by Russia in the 1950s and reproduced by the Red Chinese as Type 56, is today considered obsolete. No longer in production from the Soviets, it is still widely issued to rear-echelon troops throughout the Warsaw Pact and plays an active role in many Third World conflicts. Supplanted by the RPK in 1966, the RPD is chambered in 7.62mm, devouring 100-round belts at a cyclic rate of 700 rounds per minute.

While U.S. fighting men were making gains against the Kaiser and the Axis powers, and laying down their lives to frustrate communism in the East, a different kind of war was under way at home. From Prohibition to the present day, a "war on crime" has escalated in the streets, to reach a point where law enforcement officers complain that they are both outnumbered and outgunned by their opponents. It is time for us to meet the various combatants in that war and learn a bit about the hardware they employ.

COPS AND ROBBERS

If you are writing mysteries or action novels, chances are you'll have to deal with law enforcement personnel before you put your manuscript to bed, and if you're working on police procedurals, they're downright unavoidable. Unlike the British "bobbies," who have armed themselves but lately in response to terrorism, American peace officers have been packing iron on their hips—or on their ankles, underneath their arms, wherever—for the past two hundred years. Their adversaries, likewise, have historically respected firepower, from Captain Lightfoot and the James gang on to Dillinger, Capone, the Crips, and Bloods.

In short, when there are cops and crooks around, you're bound to find some guns. It's simply unavoidable, and while the two opposing sides have blasted one another through the years with everything from flintlocks to bazookas, pistols have remained the basic weapon in their endless conflict. Military minds have relegated side arms to the status of an afterthought, pursuing faster, better rifles, but the average lawman does his killing (and his dying) at a range of thirty feet or less. From Dodge City and the O.K. Corral to the latest Miami cocaine wars, the pistol has been and remains his first line of defense.

The Modern Wheelgun

We begin our survey with revolvers, as the six-gun dominated law enforcement for a century and still hangs on, despite the inroads made by semiautomatic pistols since the latter 1970s. Before we move along, I must reiterate a simple fact of life: with the exception of the freak Webley Fosbery "automatic revolver" [discussed in Chapter 4] wheelguns do not — I repeat, *do not* — have safeties. Authors who acquire their "knowledge" by examining the pictures in a book may answer that they've noticed *something* on the left-hand side of modern six-guns that *appears* to be a safety switch, but they are leaping to erroneous conclusions. The release catch for a swing-out cylinder is normally positioned thus, for the convenience of right-handed shooters, and nothing else on the weapon even resembles a safety. Case closed.

Unlike the frontier marshal's side arm, which was nearly always single-action, modern law enforcement uses only double-action six-guns. Double-action never caught on in the Old West, but the U.S. navy adopted its first double-action Colts in 1889, with the army following suit three years later. From a law enforcement viewpoint, double-action pieces are superior in rate of fire and in reloading, since the introduction of a swing-out cylinder with simultaneous ejection. Accuracy, on the other hand, may suffer from the double-action's longer trigger pull, which tends to drag a gun off target, but the problem is negated in the vast majority of law enforcement killing situations, which occur at point-blank range.

The modern six-gun cartridge has evolved across a span of ninety years to reach its present situation, starting with the introduction of the .45 Long Colt cartridge in 1873. Favored by Western peace officers through the turn of the century, the Colt .45 generates an average muzzle velocity of 860 feet per second, with sufficient one-shot stopping power to put a man down and keep him there.

The .38 Long Colt, introduced a year later, was noticeably

weaker at some 730 feet per second, but the U.S. military bought it anyway, refusing to acknowledge the mistake while soldiers were annihilated in the Philippines. Meanwhile, in 1897, Colt had introduced the first top-quality solid-frame double-action revolver in its New Service .45, a weapon that retained the largest frame of any U.S.-made revolver prior to introduction of the .44 Magnum. When they finally saw the light, in 1909, the army bought New Service models by the thousands, and the model also surfaced in civilian hands.

The popular .38 Special was introduced in 1902, as a replacement for the .38 Long Colt, and it eventually became standard issue for the vast majority of American police. Generating an average muzzle velocity of 900 feet per second, the new .38 (actually .357 caliber) still reigns hands-down as the world's most prolific centerfire revolver cartridge. On the down side, some authorities complain of deficits in stopping power, with suspects retaining mobility after several hits. The .38 has been particularly ineffective versus dopers high on PCP and other drugs that override the nervous system, dulling pain as they bestow inhuman strength.

An elongated version of the obsolete .44 Russian cartridge, the .44 Special was introduced in 1907, designed as an intermediate round between the .38 Special and Colt .45. Slower than the .38, at 755 feet per second, the .44 makes up in bulk what it lacks in velocity, delivering 310 foot-pounds of energy versus the .38's 179 foot-pounds.

Introduced in 1935, the mighty .357 Magnum held honors for two decades as the world's most powerful handgun cartridge. Incorporating faster-burning rifle (versus pistol) powder as propellant, the .357 develops a sizzling muzzle velocity of 1,550 feet per second, generating an average 535 foot-pounds of energy. Ideal for blowing holes in vehicles (including engine blocks), the piece became a special favorite of highway patrol officers and state troopers. On the side, it was also stockpiled by FBI agents and others who found that the magnum would penetrate many a "bulletproof" vest. Because their calibers are actually identical, .357 Magnum revolvers will also fire the smaller .38 Special cartridge. (But the .38 will not — repeat, will not — accommodate .357s!)

After twenty-one years of supremacy, the .357 was edged off its throne in 1956 by the arrival of a monster cartridge dubbed the

.44 Magnum. If you've ever watched a "Dirty Harry" film, you've seen the .44 in action, pushing law and order toward a new frontier of firepower. For the record, it's unlikely that a single shot will "blow your head clean off," but why take chances? Slower than the sleek .357, at 1,470 feet per second, the .44 Magnum still crushes the competition, delivering 971 foot-pounds of energy at the muzzle. If you want to give your wrist and ears a break, the magnum also does just fine with lighter .44 Special rounds.

The last significant addition to our list of modern six-gun cartridges was introduced in 1964. Designed as an intermediate step between the .357 and massive .44, the .41 Magnum delivers a muzzle velocity of 1,050 feet per second. While neither of the larger magnums was created with police in mind — and use of either round in categorically prohibited by major law enforcement agencies — they still show up extensively in fiction and occasionally on the street. Some small departments give their officers carte blanche in choice of hardware, and the larger magnums are a favorite choice of macho types who don't mind carrying an extra pound or so of steel.

Five major manufacturers produce revolvers of the quality required for law enforcement service. Colt and Smith and Wesson clearly dominate the field, with some departments ordering their officers to buy no other brands, but decent guns are also made by Ruger, Charter Arms, and Dan Wesson. For a more detailed review of their various offerings, outlined below, check out the latest edition of *Shooter's Bible*, issued annually by Stoeger Publishing Company.

Colt presently manufactures no .41-, .44-, or .45-caliber revolvers in double action. Their .38 Special offerings include three shorties — the Detective Special, Agent, and Commando Special — which resemble one another closely with their six-shot cylinders and 2-inch barrels. The Diamondback, another .38, is sold with either 4- or 6-inch barrels, featuring a vented rib designed to aid in dissipating heat. The Colts are sturdy and reliable and have cylinders that rotate clockwise in their frames.

The Smith and Wesson line is more prolific, starting small with Model 31, a weapon chambered for the .32 Smith and Wesson long cartridge. Catalog designation as the Regulation Police model is deceptive, since no American department uses .32-caliber side arms, and this particular cartridge—with a muzzle velocity of 705 feet per second—has little to offer in terms of stopping power. It is certainly no improvement on the .38 Special, though its 2- and 3-inch barrel options make for fair concealment as a backup weapon.

Smith and Wesson makes at least eleven "different" revolvers chambered for the .38 Special cartridge, starting with the Model 36 Chief's Special. A five-shot snubby, sold with 2- or 3-inch barrels, it is also cast in stainless steel and dubbed the Model 60. On the lighter side, a Chief's Special Airweight offers the same barrel lengths, tipping the scales at 14 ounces, versus the "fat" Special's 19 ounces. Advertised as Model 38, the Bodyguard Airweight is another five-shot weapon with a 2-inch barrel, featuring a shrouded hammer to eliminate the possibility of snags on clothing. Model 49, the Bodyguard, closely resembles Model 38, but it bulks up to 20 ounces, over the Airweight's 14.5 ounces. (A stainless Model 649 is otherwise identical to Model 49.)

In larger .38s, Smith and Wesson offers the Model 10 Military & Police revolver, with 2-, 3-, or 4-inch barrels. The identical stainless-steel version is designated Model 64, while Model 12—the Military & Police Airweight—shaves 11.5 ounces in weight, offering 2- and 4-inch barrels only. Finally, the Model 15 Combat Masterpiece (and its Model 67 stainless clone) is sold in barrel lengths of 2, 4, 6, and 8.38 inches.

Smith and Wesson offers at least seven revolvers in .357 Magnum, including the familiar crop of look-alikes and stainless-steel copies. The Model 13 Military & Police weapon is available with 3- and 4-inch barrels, its stainless version designated Model 65. The Model 19 and Model 66 Combat Magnums are likewise twinned (the latter being stainless steel), with barrel lengths of 2.5, 4, and 6 inches. Model 27 is a somewhat larger weapon, sporting 4-, 6-, and 8.37-inch barrels. The Model 28 Highway Patrolman is available in barrel lengths of 4 and 6 inches, while Smith and Wesson's top of the line, the Model 586 Distinguished Combat Magnum, offers 4-, 6-, and 8.37-inch barrels on demand.

Hauling out the big guns, Smith and Wesson advertises its Model 25, chambered for the .45 Colt cartridge, with barrels measuring 4, 6, and 8.37 inches. Model 29 (and stainless Model 629) is "Dirty Harry's" classic .44 Magnum, with barrel length of 4, 6, 8.37, and 10.63 inches. (The longer barrels are reserved primarily for target matches and hunting.) Model 57 and the stainless Model 657, meanwhile, are chambered in .41 Magnum, offering barrels of 4, 6, and 8.37 inches in length.

We can relax now, as no other manufacturer presents such a bewildering array of hardware. Ruger's Speed Six and Service Six revolvers are available in either .38 Special or .357 Magnum, with 2.75- and 4-inch barrels, while the GP-100 is chambered for .357 only, sporting barrels of 4 and 6 inches. The mighty Redhawk, variously bored to handle .357, .41, and .44 Magnum rounds, is a certified man-stopper with 5.5- and 7.5-inch barrels available.

Charter Arms manufactures their Undercover revolver in .32 Smith and Wesson Long, with a 2-inch barrel, but the five-shot Undercover .38 (with 2- or 3-inch barrel) is more likely to be chosen as a lawman's weapon. The Off-duty .38 Special is also designed with concealment in mind, its cylinder reduced to hold five shots instead of the traditional six. A larger .38 is the 4-inch Police Bulldog, while its big brother, the Bulldog "Tracker," is chambered in .357 Magnum, sporting barrels of 2.5, 4 or 6 inches. At Charter's top of the heap, the Bulldog .44 Special carries five rounds with guaranteed punch. The Special rounds won't match a magnum's killing power, but they worked just fine for Son of Sam in Queens, and Tom Harris arms his hero with a Bulldog .44 in the classic thriller, *Red Dragon*.

We don't have space available to cover all the thirty-odd revolvers manufactured by Dan Wesson in .38 Special, .357, .41, and .44 Magnum calibers. Suffice it to say that these revolvers are uniformly excellent, with a unique provision for interchangeable sights, grips, and barrels (available in lengths of 2.5, 4, 6, 8, and 10 inches). The owner of a Dan Wesson Pistol Pac can switch barrels at will, making one weapon cover a wide range of needs from concealability to long-range stopping power. On the flip side of the law, a heavy might employ the system to defeat firearms identification tests by changing barrels after an assassination, making it impossible to link his weapon with the crime.

"Automatic" Options

While the U.S. military formally adopted "automatic" pistols in 1911, sticking by them ever since, police have made the move reluctantly, without cohesive leadership. Some federal prohibition agents packed the big Colt .45 in their pursuit of whiskey runners, shooting first and asking questions later (if at all), but no significant defection from revolvers would be seen among American police until the 1970s. Constrained by civic budgets and indoctrinated in traditional beliefs of six-gun "natural superiority," police departments started shifting gears when it became apparent that their opposition was prepared to make full use of new firearms technology. Most law enforcement agencies in the United States *still* use revolvers (or allow their officers a narrow range of options), but the trend toward semiautomatic arms is plainly here to stay.

The "automatic" pistol has a number of distinct advantages in any showdown with the six-gun. Higher rates of fire and swift reloading with a simple magazine (instead of six loose bullets) are the street officer's primary concern, evoking horror stories of patrolmen shot and killed while they were trying to reload revolvers in the heat of combat. At the same time, automatics generally possess a greater ammo capacity, with staggered-line box magazines doubling — or even tripling — the six-gun's load. (A number of the better automatics also feature locking slides which let a shooter know, in no uncertain terms that he is out of ammunition.) The design of automatic pistols makes them more compact than wheelguns, and more comfortable. At the same time, automatic mechanisms eliminate gas leakage and dangerous bullet shavings that may result from misalignment of a revolver's cylinder.

With all that said, it's only fair to discuss the automatic's weaknesses. For openers, self-loading pistols universally demand a higher quality of ammunition. Underpowered rounds and misfires stop an automatic cold, whereas the shooter armed with a revolver merely has to pull the trigger one more time. Magazines are also a weak point in automatic pistols, with spring deterioration or other damage stalling the feed. Ejection of empty cases may be inconvenient, even dangerous, with hot brass flying in your partner's face (or dropping down his collar) to distract him from the job at hand. Finally, double-action six-guns often score a quicker first shot than the automatic, which traditionally fires its first shot in the single-action mode, with a shooter compelled to manually cock the hammer. (The last objection is effectively eliminated by development of double-action automatic pistols, and the common practice of carrying single-action automatics "cocked and locked" — that is, with a round in the chamber, the hammer cocked, and the safety set to prevent accidental firing.)

The modern trend toward automatic pistols was dramatized in early 1988, when spokesmen for the Drug Enforcement Administration announced the recall of the standard six-guns issued to their agents in the field. Confronted with superior firepower on every side, DEA agents received crash training with 9mm pistols and modern assault rifles, hopefully boosting their odds of survival. Elsewhere, revolvers have been replaced due to mechanical failure. In March 1988, Indianapolis police discarded their Smith and Wesson Model 586 Distinguished Combat Magnums after repeated complaints of "quality control problems," including unexplained cylinder jams under life-and-death conditions. Sgt. James Meyer's revolver jammed twice in a shootout with a felony suspect, his life spared only when the criminal ran out of ammunition. Meanwhile, on the practice range, at least two officers were cut by bullet shavings from the Smith and Wesson, one with fragments lodging in his eye.

Despite their years of service with the military, Colt automatics had no luck at all with civilian police. As noted earlier, some federal agents used the M1911A1 during Prohibition and the roundup of Depression era desperadoes, but the big .45 turned up more often in criminal hands, complete with extended 20-round magazines and occasional conversion to full-auto fire. ("Baby Face" Nelson used a converted Colt to kill one federal agent and wound two others near Rheinlander, Wisconsin, in 1933.) Modern-day commercial versions of the classic .45 include the Combat Commander, Lightweight Commander, Gold Cup National Match, and the Government Model. All carry seven rounds of .45 ammo in their magazines, with the Combat Commander and Government Model also offered in .38 Super and 9mm Luger (sporting nine-round magazines).

Smith and Wesson's several automatics offer double-action first-shot capability, and they were first to break the six-gun barrier with sales to law enforcement agencies. S&W's Model 439 is chambered in 9mm with an eight-round magazine, while Models 469 and 669 (the latter in stainless steel) offer a 12-round capacity. Model 459 and its stainless clone, Model 659, each pack fourteen 9mm rounds into their staggered-line box magazines. At the heavy end of the scale, and generally ignored by police, Model 645 is chambered in .45 caliber, with an eight-round magazine.

The Beretta Model 92 series includes some excellent 9mm automatics, and the 92F was guaranteed instant fame when it replaced the Colt .45 as America's standard military side arm in January 1985. Boasting a 15-round magazine, the Beretta weighs in at 2.52 pounds fully loaded, measuring 8.54 inches overall. Its average muzzle velocity of 1,280 feet per second easily outshines the .38 Special's performance, bordering on competition with the .357 Magnum. Making its Hollywood debut with Mel Gibson in *Lethal Weapon*, the Beretta was a fair choice for the title role.

Browning offers automatic pistols in both single and double action, the latter packing fourteen rounds in its magazine while the former settles for a mere thirteen. The classic piece is Browning's M1935 Hi-Power in single action, selected for personal backup by New York detective Frank Serpico when he prepared to blow the whistle on police corruption in Manhattan. When an abusive colleague flashed a knife at Serpico, Frank flashed the Browning, and his point was made. Tipping the scales at 2.1 pounds, the standard Browning measures 7.75 inches overall.

The Sig Sauer line of automatic pistols also features double-action capability across the board. The basic Model 220 is available in three calibers: 9mm and .38 Super versions carry nine rounds in their magazines, while the .45-caliber settles for seven. Model 225 is revised to carry eight rounds of 9mm Parabellum ammo, and its grown-up cousin, Model 226, packs fifteen rounds.

The Bren Ten automatic pistol used by Sonny Crockett on "Miami Vice" is an impressive piece of hardware to behold, but its reliance on the relatively new 10mm cartridge lets the shooter in for some potential problems. Heralded in industry releases as a cartridge that combines the stopping power of a .45 with the .357 Magnum's penetration, 10mm rounds are not widely available through normal commercial outlets. The round's future remains uncertain, but Colt is obviously banking on potential sales, with a new 10mm automatic designed to compete with the Bren Ten.

Until the 1980s, six-gun loyalists were quick to note that automatics could not handle magnum loads, and thus the automatics lost out to the revolver where raw power was concerned. A short-lived Automag, developed in the 1970s, was too expensive and erratic in performance to attract a major following, especially since the shooter was required, in many cases, to produce the rimless ammunition on his own, by amputating and reloading rifle cartridges. The ultimate solution, offered by Israeli manufacturers, has been the Desert Eagle automatic, chambered in both .357 and .44 Magnum for serious handgun enthusiasts. Measuring 10.25 inches overall, weighing 3.75 pounds when empty, the Desert Eagle feeds a nine-round magazine in .357 and seven rounds in .44-caliber. Innovative design allows the weapon to use standard revolver cartridges, rims and all, thus eliminating the need for impractical home manufacture of special rounds.

Whether lawmen carry six-guns or automatics, most urban departments mandate uniformity in selection of side arms. Striking a balance between stopping-power and public safety, the brass come down hard on officers who carry freak calibers and oversized guns on the street. Dramatic license lets your characters ignore the regulations now and then, but bear in mind the fact that fictional rogues like Dirty Harry Callahan, blasting away with his .44 Magnum in the heart of downtown San Francisco, wouldn't last ten seconds before a real-life shooting review board. (Another reason for conformity is found in combat situations, where a group of officers may be compelled to share their ammunition in the crunch. If one is firing .38s, another .44s and so on, teamwork doesn't stand a chance.)

Scatterguns in Action

While the lawman's basic weapon is (and probably will always be) his side arm, most fall back on shotguns for those killing situations that require a little "something extra" in the way of firepower. Shotguns are now carried as standard equipment in most patrol cars, and I've even seen them mounted on a few police motorcycles, in updated versions of the old saddle holster. Step into the waiting room of any urban precinct house, and chances are you'll find the duty officers working behind "bulletproof" screens, with shotguns standing by their desks or mounted on the walls.

The modern combat shotgun is designed to fill a yawning void in military/police firepower. Field experience has made it clear that average soldiers and policemen take no prizes in the field of marksmanship. Despite their training and the periodic "qualification" required of most officers, they tend to miss moving targets in the heat of battle. The obvious answer, then, is a gun that "aims itself" by spreading projectiles — the shot — over a wide area. Awesome killers at close and medium range, shotguns strike a happy balance by eliminating the risk of stray bullets cutting down distant, innocent targets.

Since the combat introduction of the Winchester M1897 in the Philippine campaign, military/police shotguns have generally been 12-gauge slide-action (pump) models. Easy to operate, reliable in action, and simple to clear in the rare event of a misfire, pump guns remain the standard shotgun choice of armies and police agencies the world over. Only in the past ten years or so have semiautomatic and revolving models made their mark with law enforcement, and we will consider two of those below, as well.

First to fight were the Winchester shotguns, pioneering the field with the venerable M1897 "trench gun." [See Chapter 4.] The Winchester Model 12 saw extensive action in World War II, primarily in the Pacific theater of operations, and it has evolved into the popular Defender series of paramilitary guns. Chambered in 12 gauge, the basic Defender sports an 18-inch barrel, with tubular magazines holding six or seven rounds. The weapon's finish is normally blued or Parkerized, except in Police and Marine models. The Defender Police shotgun is manufactured in stainless steel only, while the Marine wears a special chrome plating to resist corrosion. Both of the latter models have a slightly shortened magazine, with a maximum capacity of six rounds.

Remington's Model 870 remains one of the world's most widely used military/police shotguns, manufactured in various models including the 870R (riot) and 870P (police). A 21-inch barrel and seven-round magazine are standard, but a much shorter version, complete with pistol grip and folding metal stock, is carried by the Presidential protection detail of the U.S. Secret Service.

Ithaca shotguns are likewise well established with law enforcement agencies around the country, modern issues evolving from the Ithaca 37, widely used in World War II. Loading and ejecting shells through the same port, positioned below the receiver, 12-gauge Ithacas eliminate the problem of spent cases flying over an officer's shoulder, distracting (or blinding) his comrades. A direct descendant of the Ithaca 37, the LAPD model sports an

18.5-inch barrel, five-round magazine, and rubber butt pad for the shooter's added comfort. Ithaca's Model DS (deer slayer) comes complete with rifle-style open sights and a mandatory 20-inch barrel. On the other end of the scale, we find the Ithaca Stakeout, available in 12- or 20-gauge with five-round magazine, its pistol grip and stubby 13.23-inch barrel making for superb concealment.

Ithaca's monster shotgun — and one of the rare semiautomatic models in use by law enforcement — is the Mag-10 Roadblocker. (As a self-loader, it is also the only Ithaca that ejects spent cases through the receiver's right-hand side.) Chambered for the mighty 10-gauge cartridge, fitted with a 22-inch barrel, the weapon weighs in at 10.74 pounds, providing a rubber butt pad to soften its powerful recoil. The Roadblocker's name is self-explanatory, and the gun lives up to the designer's intent, delivering projectiles with sufficient force to ventilate the body of an average car or truck and still raise bloody hell inside. To paraphrase the armorer in *Dr. No*, this weapon only holds three rounds, but by the time they're gone, someone's been killed.

Another popular line of shotguns, the Mossberg 500 series, made its debut in 1961, working hard to crack a police market dominated by the big-name manufacturers. Sturdy and reliable, the Mossbergs are available with standard shoulder stocks and in the shorter Bullpup 12 configuration, featuring a pistol grip, 20-inch barrel, and six- or eight-round magazine.

The SPAS Model 12 (Special Purpose Automatic Shotgun) is an Italian import, manufactured with a folding metal stock and seven-round tubular magazine. As originally introduced, the SPAS combines traditional slide and self-loading actions, with a button on the forearm allowing the shooter to select his mode of preference. This revolutionary concept was apparently too much for some shooters to grasp, and variant forms of the weapon are now available in more conventional pump (MAG 12) and semiauto (LAW 12) configurations.

Based on the South African Armsel Striker design, the semiautomatic Street Sweeper boasts a 12-round revolving drum magazine and folding metal butt. Vaguely reminiscent of a classic Tommy gun with its dual pistol grips, the Street Sweeper is available with 12- and 18-inch barrels, the latter available for sale to civilians without legal restrictions. Reportedly able to empty its drum in three seconds, this rapid-fire piece has found a home with FBI SWAT teams and U.S. Border Patrol agents, entering the civilian market as an intimidating home-defense weapon.

One major advantage of using a shotgun is the variety of ammunition presently available. *Buckshot* remains the standard anti-personnel choice, with the big 00 ("double-ought") rounds packing twelve .33-caliber pellets in a single cartridge, but other loads are equally lethal. Vietnam impressed the U.S. military with a need for greater range on shotgun rounds, resulting in the introduction of *flechettes* (small, dart-like finned projectiles) capable of piercing a flack jacket at 400 yards. *Birdshot* is sometimes used to disperse rowdy mobs, but the results can be embarrassing, as at the Berkeley "People's Park" demonstrations of 1969. (One demonstrator was blinded for life; another was rushed into surgery with pellets embedded in his heart.) Solid, one-ounce *rifled slugs* convert the smooth-bore shotgun to a kind of super-rifle, capable of cracking cinder blocks, although effective range is still reduced. The special *Shok Lock* round, produced by Accuracy Systems in Phoenix, consists of a metal-ceramic projectile designed for opening locked doors, vaporizing on impact to eliminate lethal fragments.

Rifles

As in military service, when a modern lawman reaches for a rifle there are choices to be made, in terms of suitability and designated purpose. Is he facing down a gang of terrorists? About to storm a fortified Hell's Angels clubhouse? Pinning down a sniper in the middle of an urban riot zone? As different circumstances call for variations in the armed response, so law enforcement personnel are called upon to choose from various competing makes and models in their search for lethal hardware.

Assault rifles are an integral part of the modern police arsenal, with many departments using the standard M16A1 or its carbine version, the CAR 15. [See Chapter 4.] A similar design, the Armalite AR-18, is also chambered in 5.56mm, devouring 20-, 30-, or 40-round box magazines at a full-auto cyclic rate of 800 rounds per minute. Featuring selective fire capability and a folding plastic stock, the Armalite weighs in at 7.67 pounds with a loaded 20-round magazine. Used by LAPD officers in their 1974 shootout with the Symbionese Liberation Army, the AR-18 is also a favorite of Provisional IRA snipers in Belfast.

Introduced in 1973, the Ruger Mini-14 got a major publicity break ten years later, with its weekly appearance in episodes of the "A-Team" television series. Chambered in 5.56mm, the standard Mini-14s are semiautomatic weapons, feeding 10-, 20-, or 30-round box magazines. Weighing 6.83 pounds with wooden butt and a loaded 20-round magazine, the Mini-14 is also available with pistol grip and folding metal stock. A fully automatic version, designated as the Ruger AC-556, has recently been made available for use by law enforcement personnel and private security firms.

German manufacturers Heckler & Koch offer a full range of modern assault rifles, with their G3A3 model chambered in 7.62mm, weighing 11.08 pounds with a full 20-round magazine. The G3A3's cyclic rate of 500 to 600 rounds per minute is rivaled by the HK 33, chambered in 5.56mm, and both weapons are also available to the general public in modified semiautomatic versions.

Seen from time to time on NBC's "Miami Vice," the Steyr 5.56mm AUG resembles something from the set of "Star Trek," with its folding forward pistol grip, a built-in scope, and see-through plastic magazine protruding from the buttstock. Constructed on the "bull pup" design, with trigger mechanism forward of the magazine, the AUG weighs 9.02 pounds fully loaded (with a 30-round box magazine) and fires at a cyclic rate of 650 rounds per minute. Available accessories permit the arm's conversion to a launcher for riot-control and antipersonnel grenades.

When snipers start to zero in on their targets, rapid fire must yield to pinpoint accuracy, making each shot count. For counter-sniper missions, lawmen normally rely upon civilian hunting rifles fitted out with telescopic sights, but there are also "special" weapons in the field, as we shall see.

Across the country, numerous police departments utilize some version of the Remington 700 bolt-action series. Officially adopted by Marine Corps snipers in 1966, christened the M40, Remingtons are available in a wide range of calibers, including the popular .30-06 Springfield and .270 Winchester. (The latter received mixed reviews for its performance during the Attica prison revolt of September 1971, with nine hostages listed among forty persons killed by state police snipers.) Depending on the caliber selected, Remingtons offer a magazine capacity of four or five rounds.

The bolt-action Savage 110 series offers a five-round capacity in various calibers, ranging from .243 to the 7mm Remington Magnum, a big-game round generating 3,221 foot-pounds of energy, with an average muzzle velocity of 3,110 feet per second. That's a man-stopper in anybody's language, but the real big guns are yet to come.

Winchester's Model 70 series offers another line of bolt-action hunting rifles in various calibers, with magazines holding three or five rounds. The larger the cartridge, the fewer a weapon can hold, and Winchester's .458 Magnum easily qualifies in the big-game category. An "elephant" cartridge, used briefly by Clint Eastwood in *Dirty Harry*, the .458 Magnum sizzles along at 2,040 feet per second, generating some 4,620 foot-pounds of energy.

You want more? Coming up, at the top of the line in sporting arms, the Weatherby Mark V offers the usual range of calibers in bolt-action, carrying three to five rounds in its magazine, but the star of the show is a .460 Magnum round, generating an incredible 8,095 foot-pounds of energy with a muzzle velocity of 2,700 feet per second. In case there's any doubt, one hit with either of the mighty magnums just described will definitely put your man away, and even minor flesh wounds ought to set him spinning like a top.

But if you *really* want the big guns. . . .

We discussed the Browning .50-caliber machine gun earlier, in Chapter 4, but its impressive cartridge has been lately drafted into service with a pair of sniper rifles guaranteed to leave your shoulder aching . . . and your target stone-cold dead. The Barrett Model 82 Light Fifty is a semiautomatic weapon, weighing 35 pounds with its tripod and 11-round detachable box magazine. Its muzzle break allegedly reduces recoil by 30 percent, but you should still expect a pounding if you use the gun in rapid fire. The Barrett's competition, from American Military Arms, is dubbed the Long Range Rifle System, a bolt-action single-shot piece weighing 34 pounds. Either piece will drop a charging elephant, but if your accuracy leaves a bit to be desired, I'd recommend the Barrett with its extra rounds in place.

As sniping calls for special weapons, so it also calls for special training and techniques. If you have ever passed within a hundred yards of any high school physics class, you know that bullets don't fly arrow-straight forever; gravity and friction start to tamper with the flight path microseconds after firing, and a bull's-eye may be sacrificed to wind, humidity, a driving rain, or rising heat waves. Even in the best of possible conditions, snipers must allow for "rise" and "drop" before they waste a shot and give themselves away.

Let's look at an example. If you're firing .270 Winchester rounds from a 24-inch barrel, with your weapon "zeroed-in" at 250 yards, you can expect your bullets to *rise* two inches above line of sight at a range of 200 yards. The same bullet, traveling 400 yards down range, will have dropped 15.5 inches *below* line of sight, with a total drop of 36.4 inches at 500 yards.

The moral? If you're aiming at a hoodlum's nose and don't allow for physics in the bargain, you'll be lucky if you hit him in the knee. Some telescopic sights incorporate range finders to assist the marksman in his calculations, but considerable practice is required to get it right. Throw in a *moving* target at 500 yards, and we're talking major mathematics just to calculate the drop. At longer ranges, it's almost accidental that anyone gets killed.

Submachine Guns

The granddaddy of American submachine guns is the venerable Thompson [Chapter 4]. Available for sale to private citizens throughout the 1920s, "Tommy guns" were boosted by an advertisement featuring a cowboy, furry chaps and all, intent on blasting mounted rustlers from the saddle. Cities that required a special license for the ownership of handguns found the Thompson selling briskly in compliance with prevailing law, and Prohibition syndicates were quick to take advantage of the weapon.

Typically, Chicago led the way, with introduction of the Tommy gun to bootleg warfare in the fall of 1925. It would not reach Detroit until the spring of 1927, when the Purple Gang employed at least one Thompson in the Collingwood Apartments massacre, and mafioso Frankie Yale was first to feel the weapon's bite in New York City, during 1928. We have no tally for the Thompson's gangland body count, but all its other outings paled beside the 1929 St. Valentine's Day Massacre, with seven members of the Bugs Moran gang falling in a blaze of automatic fire.

The Great Depression thrust another breed of desperado into breathless headlines, with John Dillinger, Ma Barker, and a host of others packing Thompsons as they looted banks along the Midwest corridor. Following the "Kansas City Massacre" of June 1933 (five dead, two wounded), Congress moved to limit private ownership of machine guns and other "gangster weapons" (silencers, sawed-off rifles and shotguns) with the National Firearms Act of 1934. By that time, of course, the hoodlums were already well armed, and any shortages were made up by looting police stations or National Guard armories.

The 1930s outlaws took to Tommy guns like children with a brand-new toy. Dillinger posed with one of his in photographs, while "Pretty Boy" Floyd preferred more practical displays, stripping his weapon of buttstock and foregrip to create a kind of super-pistol. George "Machine Gun" Kelly liked to practice on walnuts, while "Baby Face" Nelson preferred human targets, mowing down two more FBI agents in November 1934. (One of the G-men had a Thompson, too, and Nelson was hit seventeen times before he collapsed. His final words—"I think I'm hit"—remain an all-time classic understatement.)

Still, for all their fabled firepower, Tommy guns had certain shortcomings. Texas lawman Ted Hinton, shooting it out with Clyde Barrow and Bonnie Parker in 1933, watched his .45 rounds bouncing off the outlaw vehicle. Disgusted, Hinton shifted his allegiance to the mighty Browning Automatic Rifle, backing it up with a shotgun and two .45 Colts when he helped ambush Bonnie and Clyde a year later. (Barrow and John Paul Chase—a sidekick of Baby Face Nelson—also favored the BAR for running shootouts, but other outlaws rejected the piece as too heavy and awkward.)

Technically obsolete, the Thompson is still used by various police departments, and new models have lately gone into production from a firm called Auto Ordnance. Another ghost from World War II, the M3 "grease gun," [Chapter 4] reappeared with a vengeance in the early 1970s—first, in a series of racist attacks mounted against white policemen by the Black Liberation Army, and later, in the New York assassination of Mafia underboss Tommy Eboli.

The "obsolete" Smith and Wesson M76 received a boost from Hollywood in *Prime Cut*, when Lee Marvin used the weapon to kill gangster rival Gene Hackman. Still found in many police arsenals, the M76 is chambered in 9mm Parabellum, offering selective fire capabilities with a full-auto cyclic rate of 720 rounds per minute. The weapon was produced primarily from stampings and fabrications, with a folding steel stock, weighing 8.75 pounds with a full 36-round magazine.

The Heckler & Koch MP5 series weapons are chambered in 9mm Parabellum, firing at a cyclic rate of 800 rounds per minute from 15- or 30-round box magazines. Manufactured in various forms, they include the MP5A2 (with fixed plastic buttstock), the MP5A3 (with collapsible metal stock), the MP5 SD (with built-on "silencer"), the MP5 SD1 (silenced, with no buttstock), the MP5 SD2 (silenced, with a fixed buttstock), the MP5 SD3 (silenced, with collapsible metal stock), and the MP5K (12.8 inches overall, with a forward pistol grip).

Widely used in films and television dramas, the Ingram M10 (.45 or 9mm) and M11 (.380-caliber) were first produced in the mid-1960s, with barrels threaded to accommodate the Sionics suppressor. Measuring 10.59 inches overall with the wire stock collapsed, the Ingrams average 8.4 pounds with a 30-round magazine in place. Designed as "room brooms," for eradicating urban sniper nests, original Ingrams boasted a cyclic fire rate of 1,145 rounds per minute, although many have since been modified to fire in the neighborhood of 700 rpm.

Last, we have the Uzi submachine guns, manufactured by Israeli craftsmen to exacting standards in their endless war against the Arab states. Since its introduction, the compact weapon has been formally adopted by military forces from West Germany to South Africa, serving in all climates without significant problems. (Members of the Secret Service Presidential detail put their Uzis on display in March 1981, when John Hinckley shot and wounded Ronald Reagan.) Chambered in 9mm Parabellum, the original Uzi is available with a fixed wooden butt or folding metal stock, firing at a cyclic rate of 950 rounds per minute from 20-, 25-, and 32-round magazines. A smaller version, the Mini-Uzi, maintains the larger weapon's firepower while measuring a bare 14 inches overall.

The "war on crime" will never be an even battle, as the outlaws tend to take advantage of new weaponry in record time, while law enforcement lags behind, forever playing catch-up. Such is not the case, however, with our cloak-and dagger forces, where a premium is placed on innovation and the lethal arts are pushed to reach their maximum potential. Coming up: the world and weapons of our secret agents — and the other side's.

LICENSED TO KILL

Unlike their counterparts in fiction, real-life spies are generally drab and nondescript. Their work consists primarily of tedious pursuits like tapping phones or watching who goes in and out of foreign embassies, accepting envelopes from paid informers in a park and filing long reports in triplicate. You'll seldom find them skiing down a mountainside in Switzerland with killers in pursuit, or diving in the blue Caribbean for stolen nukes. And yet. . . .

For all the boredom and the busy work involved in gathering intelligence, there are occasions when a spy must travel armed, and many governments — our own included — have resorted to the politics of murder when the cause was deemed sufficient. Authors in the field of cloak-and-dagger, therefore, need to know how agents arm themselves on "black" assignments, when they have a reason to suspect that "wet work" may be imminent.

The Spy in Fiction

Secret agents are associated in the public mind with lethal gadgetry — machine guns popping out of headlights on a flashy car, knives springing from the toes of shoes, a wristwatch with a built-in wire garrote — that generally bears no relation to the working tools of real-life spies. There *are* exotic weapons out there, and we'll take a look at several in a moment, but an agent's priorities are normally concealing and transmitting information, so the bulk of gimmicky inventions will consist of hiding places (hollow books or coins, and so forth) and transmitters (compact radios and tape recorders, "cut-out" phone lines and the like). Where weapons are concerned, simplicity is often favored over space-age sound and fury.

I think it's safe to say the James Bond's weaponry has been more thoroughly examined and dissected by the media — through novels, films, and "scholarly" analyses of same — than that of any other spy in modern fiction. (In the films produced with Roger Moore, Bond's notoriety was such that an opponent once remarked, "Your reputation precedes you"! How's *that* for secrecy?) I don't intend to talk about the movies, that deviate from the novels so dramatically that some wind up in outer space, but it is helpful to examine firearms used by Bond in thirty years of service to the queen.

In Ian Fleming's first five novels, published between 1953 and 1959, Bond's main weapon is a .25-caliber Beretta automatic pistol with "skeleton grip," that is, with the grip plates removed to reduce extra bulge in a holster. His back-up piece for serious work is an unspecified Colt .45 revolver, probably the M1917 New Service model [discussed in Chapter 4]. From *Dr. No* until the end of Fleming's lifetime, Bond abandoned the Beretta — which had nearly killed him, snagging in a quick-draw situation — for the larger Walther PPK [see Chapter 5]. The Colt was likewise cast aside in favor of Smith and Wesson's .38-caliber Centennial Airweight, a five-shot "hammerless" ancestor of the modern Airweight revolvers [Chapter 6]. The combination served Bond well in seven more novels and eight short stories, although the long-barreled Colt crops up again in *Goldfinger*, concealed in a trick compartment beneath the seat of 007's car.

Times change, and when the series was resuscitated by John Gardner in 1981, Bond turned up minus his Walther, the weapon being recalled from service for jamming at "inopportune" moments. Pulling off his first new mission with a Browning Hi-Power automatic [Chapter 6], 007 draws flack from the brass for his choice of an "obsolete" weapon. Replacements include the Ruger Redhawk .44 Magnum revolver [Chapter 6] and an interesting item from Heckler and Koch, dubbed the VP70. Chambered in 9mm, tipping the scales at 2.5 pounds with its 18-round magazine in place, this is a true double-action "automatic," lacking an external hammer or any other provision for firing a first shot in single-action mode. This makes for a long trigger pull, but the VP70 carries a fringe benefit in its capability of firing three-round automatic bursts once a special holster/shoulder stock has been attached.

James Bond's appearance on the silver screen inspired a host of imitators, from Michael Caine's terse performance in *The Ipcress File* to Dean Martin's slap-happy portrayals of Matt Helm. Gadgetry got ridiculous along the way (with Helm's cigarette lighter concealing fifty-two different weapons!), but side arms retained their position as standard equipment. On the tube, the men (and girl) from "U.N.C.L.E." favored German Lugers and Walther P38s [Chapter 5], the latter dressed up with various shoulder stocks, telescopic sights, barrel extensions, and extra-long magazines, designed to make them look like space-age rifles. Enemies from "T.H.R.U.S.H.," meanwhile, packed M1 carbines fitted out with bulky infrared scopes that no one ever seemed to use.

A less pretentious version of the cloak-and-dagger game was offered in the "I-Spy" series, starring Robert Culp and future superdad Bill Cosby. When he had his druthers, Culp was armed with a Walther P38K—a short-barreled version of the classic German side arm—while his partner used the venerable .45-caliber Colt M1911A1. Converted into a series of novels by author John Tiger, the scripts suffered in translation, with our heroes compelled to use a "standard CIA-issue" .357 Magnum revolver. Worse yet, after two or three books, the magnums were magically transformed into *automatics*, jumping the gun by two decades on the invention of successful semiauto magnum handguns.

Choice of Weapons

So, if real-life spies don't run around with sci-fi hardware clanking underneath their coats, what *do* they use? For openers, we need to think about the function of a secret agent, his position (economically, as well as geographically), and his or her intended mission.

Weapons carried on the job are tools, not cherished pets; they should be functional and practical, striking a balance between firepower and concealment. Your agent won't be looking for a target pistol with an 8- or 10-inch barrel, and he needs to give some thought to the availability of ammunition. Why carry a .44 Magnum in Afghanistan, when you know spare ammo will be nonexistent?

Likewise, government "deniability" may be a factor for consideration in your choice of weapons. If an agent or his side arm should be captured by the enemy, will either one be traceable to the United States (or England, Israel, France — wherever)? If your spook is traveling abroad, he may be wise to use the local standard-issue firearms, simultaneously nailing down a ready stock of ammunition and confusing the authorities if he is forced to ditch his weapon in a hurry.

Agents of the Eastern Bloc will carry Makarov 9mm automatics [Chapter 5] or older Tokarevs [see Chapter 4], but they have access to a wide variety of Western weapons on the side. The latter may be useful for assassination, when a weapon "accidentally" discarded points the finger of suspicion at the CIA, Mossad, or other hostile agencies. In Asia, spooks from China, North Korea, Laos, and Vietnam are likely to be armed with the Chinese Type 59 (Makarov) or Type 51 (Tokarev) pistols [described in Chapter 5], falling back on captured French or American weapons when deniability must be preserved.

Western Europe offers more variety in side arms. Easily the most prolific — serving in fifty nations worldwide — is the 9mm Browning Hi-Power automatic [described in Chapter 6]. Lately manufactured by Fabrique Nationale, in Belgium, the Browning has been officially adopted by that nation, plus Denmark, the Netherlands, and the United Kingdom. Other Western European nations and their standard arms include:

Austria - various Walthers, including the P38 in 9mm Parabellum;

Finland - the Lahti Model L35 in 9mm, resembling a classic Luger without the toggle mechanism;

France - (a) the 9mm MAS, weighing 2.3 pounds with its nine-round magazine in place, and (b) the Model D MAB, chambered for the 7.65mm Longue cartridge used only in France;

Italy - the Beretta 92 series [Chapter 6] and the Beretta 93R, a 9mm weapon weighing 2.47 pounds with a 15-round magazine in place, featuring selective fire capability for three-shot full-auto bursts, with a folding foregrip to steady the shooter's aim when his left thumb is hooked through the oversized trigger-guard;

Norway - the Colt .45 M1911A1 and a domestic copy, the Model 1914;

Portugal - the classic Luger Pistole 08, plus 7.62mm Savage Models 1907 and 1915, dubbed the M/908 and M/915 by Portuguese users;

Spain - the indigenous 9mm Super Star automatic, combining the Colt M1911A1's outward appearance with the internal mechanism of the Browning Hi-Power;

Sweden - the 9mm Lahti Model 1940, identical to the Finnish Lahti except for a modified mount on the recoil spring;

Switzerland - the double action Sig Sauer Pistole 75, chambered in 9mm, weighing 1.83 pounds without its nine-round magazine;

West Germany - (a) the Walther P1 in 9mm, weighing 2.11 pounds with a full eight-round magazine; (b) the lighter P5, weighing 1.95 pounds with the same 9mm load; (c) the Heckler & Koch VP 70 [described above]; and (d) the Heckler & Koch HK4, chambered in 9mm Short, available with seven- or eight-round magazines.

Third World nations are generally armed by the Americans, Soviets, or Chinese, sometimes obtaining their hardware from all three suppliers. In Latin America, .45-caliber automatics remain popular, with U.S. surplus weapons widely used. Mexico produced the Obregon .45, a straightforward copy of the Colt M1911, while Argentina manufactures Ballester Molina clones of both the M1911 and M1911A1, dubbing them the M1916 and M1927, respectively. Browning automatics are widely used in Africa, with revolutionary nations tending toward Soviet arms and their Chinese facsimiles. In the Middle East, Israel and Egypt use 9mm Berettas, while other nations draw their arms from the United States or the USSR.

The Sounds of Silence

In the world portrayed by Hollywood (and many publishers), no self-respecting spook would be caught dead without his silencer, but I suggest that you approach this area with caution. Bear in mind that all those "silent" weapons in the movies and on television have received assistance from a team of sound technicians, in a laboratory miles from where the film was made. Godzilla wasn't real, my friends, and neither are the vast majority of silencers depicted on the silver screen.

For openers, there's no such thing. In proper terms, the baffled tube attached to firearms in an effort to reduce their loud report is a *suppressor*, and the name is self-explanatory. It suppresses — but does not eliminate — the sound emitted from a firearm's muzzle. At the trial of several neo-Nazis charged with killing Alan Berg, a Jewish talk-show host in Denver, a description of the murder weapon was presented to the jury. As described by witnesses, the "silenced" Ingram submachine gun used on Berg produced a sound like someone slamming down a heavy dictionary on a desktop.

R. Lance Hill presents a fine, authentic-sounding picture of a silenced weapon in *The Evil That Men Do* (Bantam, 1978):

> Having begun life as a quite ordinary Smith and Wesson Model 57 revolver in .41 Magnum caliber, the firearm had then undergone more than a hundred hours of work in order for it to suit Holland's exacting standards: fitted with a custom five-inch barrel, muzzle vented and sufficiently heavy to reduce recoil ...
>
> Also in the case was a silencer. ... Most [are] woeful devices severely hindering the effectiveness of the firearm they are coupled to, restricting the bullet's velocity as well as adversely affecting the accuracy because of vibrations. They are deplored for fouling the gun barrel with spent powder, many not suppressing the report of the gun so much as redirecting the noise indiscriminately. However, the suppressor Holland employed was the latest in applied technology and not only did all that a suppressor was designed to do, but in practice actually enhanced the velocity of the bullet passing through its titanium embrace.

Convinced? Unfortunately, Hill is wrong across the board. For starters, it's impossible to "silence" a revolver, since the sound and flash of every shot escape through open space around the cylinder. Next problem: the description of a "vented" barrel simply means there have been holes cut near the muzzle, to reduce a weapon's kick. If vents are covered by a silencer, they do no good, and if they're *not*, the sound of every shot escapes as if there were no silencer attached. To round things off, Hill has a basic problem with his choice of ammunition. Many bullets travel faster than the speed of sound, like tiny fighter planes, and make another racket independent of their weapon once they leave the muzzle. No attachment can suppress this secondary noise, and so the active candidates for silencing are limited to guns that fire projectiles at subsonic speeds — that is, slower than 1,100 feet per second. The average .41 Magnum round has a muzzle velocity of 1,500 feet per second, and Hill's technology makes it travel even *faster*, indicating that his super-gun would probably be loud enough to wake the dead.

(I won't say that suppressors cannot be *attached* to a revolver. French police recovered one such weapon when they gunned down gangster Jacques Messrine, in 1979, and others undoubtedly exist. They just don't *work*.)

Another author who plays fast and loose with "silent" guns is best-seller Robert Ludlum. In novels like *The Aquitaine Progression* and *The Chancellor Manuscript*, Ludlum consistently describes his suppressors as "perforated tubes," which logically should let the pent-up gas — and sound — escape each time the piece is fired. The muffled "spits" which emanate from Ludlum's Swiss-cheese silencers, on paper, bear no similarity to the ungodly racket such a weapon would produce in combat.

In summary, any pistol meant to function with a "silencer" should be a semiautomatic weapon, chambered for subsonic ammunition. Likely candidates include the .25, .32, .380, and .45-caliber automatic rounds, with muzzle velocities ranging from 760 to 990 feet per second in various loads. Professional killers often favor a .22-caliber automatic like the Ruger Mark II, fired at skin-touch range, the suppressor muffling detonation while their target soaks up the muzzle blast.

Restricted by federal law since 1934, "silencers" are professionally manufactured for military use and sale to friendly governments, with some weapons—like the Heckler & Koch MP5 SD submachine guns—having suppressors installed at the factory. In the United States, would-be commandos may circumvent the law by purchasing suppressor components in kit form (complete with printed warnings against assembling same!) or by rigging some homemade device of their own. The rubber nipple of a baby's bottle, fastened to the muzzle of a .22-caliber weapon, provides fair suppression for two or three shots, and professional killer Joe (The Animal) Barboza reportedly used truck mufflers to "silence" an M1 Garand rifle. In the early 1980s, threaded adapters were offered for sale, permitting substitution of plastic soft-drink bottles for the Sionics suppressors normally used on Ingram submachine guns.

The Assassination Game

Since 1865, most infamous political assassinations have been executed with revolvers, fired at point-blank range, but it requires a kamikaze-type mentality to murder in a crowd, up close and personal. Unless your character is suicidal, he will want some lag time in between the strike and enemy reaction, to effect his getaway. That brings us back to rifles, and specifically the models built for military sniping missions.

We've discussed domestic rifles [Chapter 6] and their employment by police, with mention of the MP40 Remington, in use by the United States Marines. Another U.S. sniper rifle is the M21, a modified version of the old M14 that survived the general transition from 7.62mm NATO to the 5.56mm round. A semiautomatic piece, the weapon measures 44.09 inches overall and weighs 12.24 pounds with a loaded 20-round box magazine. The average muzzle velocity for its 7.62mm rounds is 2,798 feet per second.

Austria's primary sniper rifle is the Steyr SSG 69, a bolt-action weapon chambered in 7.62mm. Measuring 44.9 inches overall, it weighs 10.14 pounds empty, feeding cartridges from a five-round rotary magazine or a ten-round detachable box. Boasting a muzzle velocity of 2,821 feet per second, the Steyr uses a Kahles ZF69 telescopic sight graduated to a range of 875 yards, scoring ten-shot groups within a 16-inch circle at maximum range.

French snipers use the FR-F2 bolt-action rifle, chambered

for either 7.5mm or 7.62mm rounds. Weighing 11.95 pounds empty, the piece measures 44.8 inches, incorporating a 10-round magazine. With an average muzzle velocity of 2,795 feet per second, the FR-F2 wears a black nylonite sleeve on its barrel, thus eliminating the problem of heat haze and potential distortion in aiming.

Britain's sniper is the L42A1, a bolt-action descendant of the old Lee-Enfield .303-caliber rifle, chambered in 7.62mm. Weighing 9.76 pounds with its ten-round magazine, the rifle measures 46.5 inches overall and achieves a muzzle velocity of 2,750 feet per second. Used in the Falklands campaign, the L42A1 deserves its reputation as an accurate long-distance killer.

Belgium's Fabrique Nationale manufactures the FN Model 30-11, a bolt-action sniper rifle chambered in 7.62mm. At 10.69 pounds, it measures 43.97 inches and carries a five-round magazine, with rounds attaining a muzzle velocity of 2,788 feet per second. Available accessories include a bipod and infrared night vision scopes.

The Galil Sniping Rifle, manufactured in Israel, is a semiautomatic weapon chambered in 7.62mm, equipped with a folding buttstock and bipod. Measuring 43.9 inches overall, it weighs 17.68 pounds with telescopic sight and 20-round box magazine, delivering rounds at an average muzzle velocity of 2,674 feet per second. Designed with battlefield reliability in mind, the Galil is built to score head shots at 300 meters, half-body hits at 600 meters, and full-figure hits at 800 to 900 meters.

Italy's Beretta Sniper is another bolt-action rifle, chambered in 7.62mm. Measuring 45.87 inches overall, the weapon weighs 15.87 pounds with five rounds in place, hurling projectiles down range at a muzzle velocity of 2,838 feet per second. The wooden forestock conceals a forward-pointing counterweight beneath the free-floating barrel, designed to reduce the natural barrel vibrations produced by firing.

West German troops employ two different rifles for sniping. One is the Mauser SP 66, a bolt-action weapon carrying three rounds of 7.62mm ammunition in its magazine. Authorities will not divulge the rifle's weight or total length, but the barrel measures 26.77 inches, delivering rounds at a muzzle velocity of 2,821 feet per second. The alternative rifle is the PSG1, from Heckler &

Koch, a semiautomatic likewise chambered for 7.62mm. Measuring 47.56 inches overall, the PSG1 weighs 17.85 pounds without its five- or 20-round box magazines. Average muzzle velocity has been recorded at 2,821 feet per second.

The "Exotics"

Various exotic weapons are the ones that come to mind when modern movie buffs and readers think of spies in action. Ian Fleming did his share to put the ball in motion, hiding guns in canes and hollow books, while Hollywood has made a fetish out of lethal gimmickry. By contrast, real-life manufacturers have lagged behind, but there are bona fide reports of guns disguised as fountain pens and other homely objects — even hidden in prosthetic limbs. One outfit builds a special briefcase "holster" for the Ingram submachine gun, with a trigger in the handle: all a shooter has to do is squeeze and spin in circles, while his lethal luggage does the rest.

In World War II, the OSS produced a "special" handgun called the Liberator for air drops behind enemy lines. Manufactured under the code name of Flare Pistol M1942, each single-shot weapon cost $2.40 to produce. Before the airlift, they were packed in see-through plastic bags, complete with ten rounds each and crude instructions printed in the form of comic strips, *sans* dialogue. On firing, it was necessary for the shooter to insert some slender object down the barrel, punching out the empty brass before he could reload. (A modern version of the Liberator, dubbed the "Deer Gun," was produced in 1964 for use in Vietnam, but records indicate that it was never issued.)

When America declared its covert war on Fidel Castro, circa 1960, CIA technicians burned the midnight oil to dream up innovative ways of knocking off "the Beard." (In one case literally, with a plan to dust depilatory powder on the Cuban's clothing.) Members of the Mafia were used to smuggle poison and a sniper's rifle into Cuba, all in vain, but Langley's finest minds were not defeated. A boxfull of poisoned cigars was prepared, then deep-sixed out of fear that they might be shared with friendly diplomats before Castro took his last smoke. LSD was suggested, to "embarrass" Fidel with a bum trip in public, and some other genius suggested high-explosive seashells, designed to kill Castro while he was skin diving. In the end, the only casualties were certain mafiosi who allowed themselves to get involved with the peculiar scheme, and Castro was allowed to live in peace.

The KGB has shown an interest in exotic weapons since the 1950s, with some interesting results. In 1954, the Moscow laboratory provided Captain Nikolai Khokhlov with assassination weapons including a three-barreled battery-powered pistol and a cigarette case concealing another electric gun. By eliminating gunpowder and using an electric charge, the Soviets had finally perfected silent shooting, counting on close range and poisoned "dum-dum" (hollow-point) bullets to guarantee a kill.

While Capt. Khokhlov had displayed no signs of squeamishness in wartime, he surprised the KGB—then known as MVD—by bolting after he was sent to kill defector Georgi Okolovich in Frankfurt. Delivering his weapons and considerable information to American authorities, Khokhlov went on the lecture circuit, denouncing Soviet subversion, and Department 13 (in charge of assassinations) issued his death warrant in 1957. That September, down while attending a conference in Frankfurt, Khokhlov was stricken down with an illness whose symptoms are graphically described by John Barron in *KGB* (Bantam, 1974).

Hideous brown stripes, dark splotches, and black-and-blue swellings disfigured his face and body. A sticky secretion oozed from his eyelids, and blood seeped through his pores; his skin felt dry, shrunken, and aflame. At the mere touch of his hand, great tufts of his hair fell out. . . . Tests on September 22 showed that Khokhlov's white corpuscles were being swiftly and fatally destroyed, his bones decaying, his blood turning to plasma, and his saliva glands atrophying.

And you thought *you* had problems! A week of round-the-clock treatments with steroids, vitamins, and experimental antidotes were combined with intravenous feeding and near-continuous blood transfusions, finally reversing the course of Khokhlov's ailment and saving his life. Analysts determined that he had been dosed with thallium, a rare toxic metal, which the Soviets had first bombarded with intense radiation, breaking the metal down into tiny particles before it was sprinkled over Khokhlov's food. Upon ingestion, he was fighting the effects of both a deadly poison and the radiation which had permeated every portion of his body.

While Khokhlov waged a silent battle for his life in Frankfurt, other Russian hit men were stalking a Ukrainian activist leader, Lev Rebet, in Munich. Their weapon was a metal tube, one half-inch in diameter and seven inches long, containing a simple firing device and a tube of deadly prussic acid. Upon detonation of a small charge, the ampule was crushed, spraying poison into the target's face. Instant constriction of blood vessels produced death, resembling a heart attack, with swift post-mortem relaxation wiping out the evidence before an autopsy. Following a practice run to test the weapon on a dog, the killers nailed Rebet on October 12, 1957. His death was diagnosed as being caused by cardiac arrest. (The same technique was used to murder Stefan Bandera, also in Munich, in October 1958. This time, authorities found traces of prussic acid in the victim's stomach, along with flakes of glass on his face, from the exploding ampule.)

One handy method of delivering a lethal dose (or tranquilizer) is by using air guns, such as those produced by Benjamin or Crossman. Normally offered in .177 and .22 caliber, these pistols and rifles used compressed air to propel pellets, darts—whatever—with a minimum of noise. (The usual report is something in the nature of a *pop*, much like the sound produced by "silenced" weapons in the movies.) Single-shot models generally feature some sort of hand pump for building up pressure, while the various repeaters utilize tubes or canisters of compressed air and carbon dioxide. Your poison darts will have to be a custom item, but the air gun's strongest point is its ability to spit out damn near anything—from rocks to ballpoint fillers—if your chosen ammunition has the right diameter.

In September 1978, after broadcasting details of Bulgarian communist party leaders' sexual habits, defector Georgi Markov fell suddenly ill in London. Within four days, he was dead, leaving doctors with a vague complaint of being jostled at a bus stop, carelessly jabbed in the leg by another passenger's umbrella. The autopsy revealed a tiny pellet embedded in Markov's thigh, once filled with Ricin, an extract from the castor-oil plant described as bearing double the toxicity of cobra venom. A similar pellet was extracted from the back of Bulgarian Vladimir Kostov, in Paris, but Kostov managed to survive after a period of critical illness.

It should not be supposed that Soviet assassins are always so subtle. In the long hunt for Leon Trotsky, at least sixteen persons were gunned down, blown up, or beaten to death before the Russians finally got their man. (One, a friend of Trotsky's son, was kidnapped and decapitated in Paris, his headless body dumped in the Seine.) A band of twenty agents armed with submachine guns, led by artist David Sequeiros, raided Trotsky's Mexican villa in May 1940, spraying his bedroom with 200 bullets before they retreated, successful only in killing an American bodyguard. Three months later, a lone assassin got lucky and finished Trotsky off with a mountaineer's ax, providing future inspiration for author Lawrence Sanders and his best-seller, *The First Deadly Sin*.

Regardless of their chosen methods, secret agents will ideally strive to kill in private, covering their tracks and shifting blame to hostile agencies — or, at the very least, securing some time to make their getaway. As we shall see in Chapter 8, the opposite holds true for terrorists, who do their killing publicly, with fanfare — hopefully on camera — in a bid to advertise their "cause."

REIGN OF TERROR

Since 1980, give or take, the modern action genre has been overrun with terrorists. They crop up everywhere, and in the past ten years or so they've forced the Mafia, Hell's Angels, street gangs, and assorted other scum to vie for second place as Menace of the Moment. This should come as no surprise to anyone who reads the daily headlines, but relax — I'm not about to resurrect the great debate about life imitating art, or vice versa. I likewise won't suggest that anyone *should* write about a terrorist conspiracy, but if you *do*, it pays to know your hardware going in.

We'll cover bombs and rockets in another chapter, but for now let's concentrate upon the firearms used most frequently by terrorists. The modern "freedom fighter" has his special favorites, like anybody else, and the selection is determined to a great extent by function and convenience. The perfect weapon should be easily concealable, yet powerful enough to drop a human target in his tracks; it should be capable of rapid fire, without excessive waste of costly ammunition. Sound familiar? If it doesn't, I suggest you take another look at Chapters 6 and 7, as we're dealing with the same criteria applied to choice of weapons for police, their outlaw adversaries, and the average secret agent.

Rifles

Unlike the average combat soldier, terrorists are seldom called upon to do their killing from a distance. Classic sniper missions are a rarity — outside of Belfast and Beirut — with most assassinations taking place at point-blank range, or in the form of drive-by shootings. Long-range weapons likewise offer poor concealment, for the most part, but the modern crop of assault rifles have managed to strike a happy balance between firepower and convenience. Folding stocks, selective fire, and stopping power far beyond the average capability of submachine guns make these weapons highly suitable for killers with a "cause."

The Russian AK 47 [Chapter 5] is easily the hands-down favorite arm of terrorists and revolutionaries everywhere. Aside from rugged quality and stopping power, the Kalashnikov is also readily available at bargain-basement prices, sometimes passed out free of charge by Moscow's missionaries from the KGB. In Vietnam, the AK 47 functioned under field conditions that produced no end of problems for the M16. Since then, it has been variously used by Palestinian guerrillas infiltrating Israel, Black September terrorists in Munich, and the IRA in Belfast. In Africa and Southeast Asia, terrorists are free to choose between the offerings of Moscow and their Chinese carbon-copies, frequently selecting some of each to keep things friendly all around.

The Czech Vz.58 assault rifle [Chapter 5] is another weapon popular with terrorists around the world. Sold commercially by Omnipol, its manufacturer, the rifle finds its way to eager hands from Tripoli to Tokyo. Three Vz.58s, with butts removed, were used by Japanese Red Army gunners — acting on behalf of the Popular Front for the Liberation of Palestine — when they shot up Tel Aviv's Lod Airport in May 1972, killing twenty-six persons and wounding another seventy-six. That "triumph" did so much for terrorist morale that one Red Army faction promptly changed its name to "Vz.58."

A favorite weapon of the Provisional Irish Republican Army

in Belfast, the Armalite AR-18 [Chapter 6], is obtained primarily from U.S. sources, smuggled into Northern Ireland to support the world's longest-running guerrilla war. Capable of penetrating helmets and body armor at 500 yards, the Armalite in Provo hands plays havoc with British patrols, and many of the semiautomatic "civilian" models have been modified to full-auto fire by IRA gunsmiths. The AR-18's folding stock allows for fair concealment under trench coats and the like, but it is often broken down for transport and delivery by designated "gun carriers," relieving valued snipers of the need to lug their own weapons around the streets.

While labeled obsolete for military purposes, the M1 carbine is still widely available throughout Latin America and the United States. Customized full-auto carbines were used by the Symbionese Liberation Army in 1974-75, and the M1 also turns up in IRA hands from time to time. A pair of carbines were among the weapons captured when police broke up the Provo Balcombe Street gang in London, during 1976. IRA gunners are fond of posing with the sporty M1 for publicity photos.

Pistols

Most terrorists, like gangsters and policemen, hate to walk around unarmed. You never know when someone from the opposition — SAS, Mossad, the FBI, whoever — may decide to take you off the street, and there are situations when an unexpected target may present itself. Let's say you're strolling through a Belfast suburb, heading for your weekly meeting of the IRA, when suddenly you glance across the street and see the Prince of Wales alighting from a taxi. What's a terrorist to do?

If he's prepared, he whips his pistol out and chalks one up for "people's liberation." Granted, he may have to cross the street, but it's a minor price to pay for glory, in the long run. Pistols are the most concealable of standard firearms, and the semiautomatic's rate of fire, combined with modern magazine capacity, lets certain handguns rival the performance of the M1 carbine in a pinch. If we include selective fire, available on models like the VP70 and the Beretta 93 R, we're looking at a mini-submachine gun that will fit inside a pocket or a lady's handbag, ready to emerge and settle any arguments that may arise.

The Russian Tokarev [discussed in Chapter 4] and Chinese

copies are available to terrorists in every Middle Eastern, African, and Asian country where the "people's forces" are at war with the establishment. One variant, the 9mm Parabellum "Tokagypt," has a peculiar history which may be worthy of discussion here. Manufactured in Hungary, the Tokagypt was offered to Egyptian President Nasser after the U.S. refused to supply him with weapons. Unimpressed with the pistol's performance, Nasser cancelled his order, leaving U.S. dealers to take up the slack by purchasing the guns at surplus prices. Tokagypt pistols bound for America were stamped with the word "Firebird," but our government rescinded necessary import licenses at the last minute, thereby dumping thousands of weapons on the European commercial market. Firebirds later became the standard side arm of Germany's Baader-Meinhof gang, with sources ranging from West German gunshops to salesmen for Al Fatah.

The modern Makarov [see Chapter 5] is found in Arab hands throughout the Middle East, and it is also popular with terrorists in Western Europe. Members of the "Carlos" gang were packing Makarovs when they invaded OPEC headquarters in Vienna on December 21, 1975, seizing hostages in expectation of a $25 million ransom. The Jackal used his gun to kill a senior member of the Libyan delegation that day, while another member of the team — Baader-Meinhof stalwart Gabrielle Krocker-Tiedemann — blazed away with two Makarovs, killing an Austrian policeman and a bodyguard assigned to the Iraqi oil minister.

The venerable Walther P38 [Chapter 5] became so popular with Italy's Red Brigades, that at one point they were publicly nicknamed the "P Thirty-eighters." Stylish, accurate, and powerful, the classic German side arm proved ideal for street abductions and assassinations, not to mention the distasteful chore of "kneecapping" critics and traitors. In 1975, the Red Brigades initiated publication of a revolutionary journal called *Mai piu Senza Fusile* — *Never Without a Gun* — which they dedicated, in spirit, to the P38.

Adopted as the official military side arm of fifty different nations, the Browning Hi-Power automatic is available to terrorists the world over. Gudrun Ensslin, of the Baader-Meinhof gang, was carrying one when she was captured by police in Hamburg. Carlos the Jackal used another Browning in his December 1973 attempt to assassinate Teddy Sieff, a London business executive and prominent Zionist. Incredibly, a classic shot was foiled when Sieff's front teeth absorbed the bullet's killing impact, leaving it to lodge within a millimeter of his jugular.

While terrorists are prone to favor automatic pistols, IRA commandos have obtained large stocks of Smith and Wesson .38 revolvers from domestic sources and the British military, using them extensively for knee-capping and street-corner assassinations. A pair of the six-guns were confiscated as part of the Balcombe Street gang's mobile arsenal. Trigger man Edward Butler, later jailed for life, refused to leave the house without his trusty Smith and Wesson. "I would not go shopping without it," he told authorities. "I carred it everywhere."

Another wheelgun favored by the sons of Erin is the Spanish Astra, chambered in .357 Magnum. Procured from allies in the Basque ETA movement, the Astra was used to execute London businessman Alan Quartermaine in 1974, with firearms identification tests linking the same gun to a raid on the Naval and Military Club that December. The Balcombe Street gang used another Astra magnum to kill Ross McWhirter, publisher of the *Guinness Book of World Records*, in 1975, after he posted a $100,000 reward for the arrest of IRA bombers then plaguing London.

A powerful Czech weapon, the M52 automatic, has become extremely popular with terrorists in Western Europe. Used as standard issue with Czech front-line units (and passed on from there to various "armies of liberation"), the M52 weighs 2.11 pounds with a loaded eight-round magazine, chambering a powerful 7.62mm bottleneck cartridge with a muzzle velocity of 1,600 feet per second. Carlos the Jackal was packing an M52 when French police tried to arrest him in June 1975 at his girlfriend's apartment on Rue Toullier, in Paris. Led by Michel Moukharbel, a traitorous liaison officer from the Popular Front for the Liberation of Palestine, officers were surprised when Carlos whipped out his side arm and started blasting at point-blank range. Two of the constables were killed and a third wounded before Carlos turned the gun on Moukharbel, dropping him in his tracks. A round fired through the victim's prostrate body pierced the floor and drilled through ceiling panels of the room downstairs, punched through a table, and buried itself so deeply in those floorboards that it could not be retrieved.

A newer weapon, manufactured in America since 1983, the Glock 17 has incited widespread controversy with allegations that it is the first "plastic gun." A Jack Anderson column, published in 1986, lamented the advent of "plastic" weapons, designed to evade airport security checks, and predicted a flood of Khaddafy-backed terrorists prowling the West, armed with Glock 17s. In fact, as manufacturers point out, the Glock is only 17 percent plastic, with its barrel and internal works constructed out of solid steel. All hype aside, the pistol is effectively concealable, measuring 7.5 inches overall, weighing 1.9 pounds with a loaded 17-round magazine. Chambered in 9mm, the Glock is capable of placing five-shot groups inside a 2.5-inch circle at a range of 25 yards.

Automatic Weapons

The classic light machine gun, based upon its size and weight, has limited appeal to modern terrorists, but there are situations where the larger weapons come in handy. Russian RPDs and Chinese copies [both discussed in Chapter 5] are used by Palestinians throughout the Middle East, and sightings of the weapon are especially frequent in Beirut. Guerrillas in Afghanistan have also turned the RPD against their Soviet opponents, chalking up a point for pure poetic justice in the process.

In 1978, a shipment of seven M60 machine guns was stolen from a National Guard armory in the United States, surfacing weeks later with IRA in Northern Ireland. By the time the weapons were displayed in Londonderry, during a parade that June, one of them had already been used to ambush three constables of the Royal Ulster Constabulary. Another M60 killed Captain Richard Westmacott, when SAS commandos raided an IRA stronghold, but six of the guns were reportedly recovered by early 1982.

Submachine guns generally have more value for terrorists, and a sentimental favorite with IRA gunmen is the obsolete Thompson [covered in Chapters 4 and 6]. Purchased in bulk during the 1920s, Tommy guns have been immortalized in Irish song, their silhouette embroidered on handkerchiefs sold at Provo fund-raising events. A few were also used by England's only native terrorist group, the so-called Angry Brigade, which collapsed after mass arrests in 1972. Stateside, Thompsons continue to circulate in the hands of police and criminals alike, breaking the color bar to win acceptance by both the Ku Klux Klan and the Black Liberation Army in the 1970s.

Britain's obsolete Sten gun [Chapter 4] is another weapon favored by the defunct Angry Brigade and certain IRA factions. One Sten, captured with the arsenal of the Balcombe Street gang, had been used in drive-by shootings of London pubs patronized by servicemen. Reliable in service, fairly cheap to copy, it is probable that Stens will have a place in Ulster's war for years to come.

The Heckler & Koch MP5 [Chapter 6] is standard issue in West Germany and thirty-four other countries. Serving almost as widely in terrorist hands as with lawful authorities. Favored by the Baader-Meinhof gang in Germany, an MP5 was sketched against the background of a five-pointed star to create an official emblem for the group's Red Army Faction. Submachine guns stolen from an armory in Switzerland were used at Cologne in September 1977 to kidnap industrialist Hans-Martin Schleyer, killing his driver and three bodyguards in the process. The MP5 is also popular with Britain's SAS commandos, who used their modified "Hocklers" in the May 1980 raid on the occupied Iranian embassy in London.

A standard weapon with Czech security forces, the Skorpion Model 61 submachine gun is also a favorite of terrorists around the world. Ideal for concealment, the Skorpion measures 10.6 inches overall with its wire butt folded, tipping the scales at 4.4 pounds with a 20-round magazine in place. Chambered in 7.65mm, the weapon has a cyclic rate of 840 rounds per minute, with a muzzle velocity of 1,040 feet per second. Efficient silencers are available for the Skorpion, and while they cut effective range in half — from 220 to 100 yards — this scarcely matters in the point-blank world of urban terrorism. The Red Brigades used a Skorpion to kill Aldo Moro in May 1978; tests showed that the same gun had earlier cut down Francesco Coco, the chief prosecutor of Genoa. Skorpions are used extensively by black hit teams in Johannesburg, and police captured one in a raid on the Jackal's Parisian hideout during June 1975. Two years later, in September 1977, another Skorpion was used in the attempted assassination of Iranian Princess Ashraf, on the French Riviera.

Designed for Italian commando units, the Beretta Model 12 submachine gun has also been sold to various nations in Africa, Latin America, and the Middle East. Chambered in 9mm Parabellum, this compact weapon measures 16.4 inches overall, weighing 8.13 pounds with a full 32-round magazine. (Magazines holding 20 and 40 rounds are also available.) Firing at a cyclic rate of 500 to 550 rounds per minute, the Beretta hurls projectiles down range at a muzzle velocity of 1,250 feet per second. Two of these weapons were used by Carlos and company in the OPEC raid of December 1975, and others have found their way into terrorist hands throughout Western Europe.

The stubby Ingram submachine guns [Chapter 6] have been sold to friendly governments in Central and South America, some inevitably winding up in rebel hands. Stateside, they are popular with neo-Nazi gunmen in their war against the "Zionist Occupational Government." Shops have been established for conversion of semiautomatic civilian weapons to full-auto fire. One such was used to murder Alan Berg, in Denver, during 1984; another, in the hands of an Aryan Nations commando, was employed to kill a black state trooper in Arkansas. Suppressors for the Ingram have been manufactured in various gun shops, including one run by a pseudoreligious hate group calling itself the Covenant, Sword, and Arm of the Lord.

Sources of Terrorist Arms

Terrorism is big business. According to published reports, the rulers of Saudi Arabia contribute $25 million each year to PLO coffers, and the organization's Wall Street portfolio was valued at $35 million in 1982. Libya's Colonel Khaddafy shelled out $40 million to Black September terrorists in 1975, before oil prices started dropping, and he still contributes an average $5 million per year to the Provisional IRA. If cash runs short, the Provos have other ways of making ends meet, such as stealing $4 million in a series of 1977 bank robberies. Stateside, banks and Brinks trucks have been looted by groups as diverse as The Order, the Aryan Nations, the Weather Underground, the Black Liberation Army, the United Peoples' Forces, and the Symbionese Liberation Army. By and large, once leaders skim their cut to cover the expense of stylish clothes and fancy cars, the money goes for guns.

In the United States, domestic terrorists need only drive around the block to find a gun store, shopping from a wide variety of paramilitary weapons in "civilian" (i.e., semiautomatic) styles.

If semiauto isn't good enough, the chances are a friendly gunsmith can be found to make the necessary alterations for a price. Abroad, the IRA has been on the receiving end of countless shipments from America, beginning in the early 1920s and continuing until the present day. The flow of cash and arms has fluctuated with events in Northern Ireland and increasing federal scrutiny on "charities" like NORAID, but if sources in the West run dry, the Provos merely shop around. (In 1971, Basque terrorists delivered fifty revolvers to Belfast, as payment for lessons in handling explosives.) Between 1970 and 1978, British authorities captured 7,000 guns and close to a million rounds of ammunition in the six counties of Northern Ireland, and their tabulation did not include shipments seized en route from the southern Republic.

The Eastern Bloc, controlled by Russia, is an endless source of arms for terrorists of every stripe around the world. In the autumn of 1971, Czech manufacturers sold 4.5 tons of weapons to the Provisional IRA, including firearms, ammunition, hand grenades, bazookas, and rocket launchers. Seized by customs authorities at Schiphol airport, the shipment filled 166 separate crates. Bulgaria has been especially generous with lethal hardware, funneling arms to the Turkish People's Liberation Army and other leftist movements in the Near East. Between 1971 and 1973, Turkish police captured 4,457 guns and 4.65 million rounds of ammunition from native terrorists, including Soviet AK 47s, pistols, and grenades; by 1977, the take had risen to 40,000 guns, nearly all from Warsaw Pact sources. In June 1977, Turkish security forces in the Bosporus raided the cargo vessel *Vasoula*, confiscating sixty-seven tons of weapons slated for delivery to leftist revolutionaries.

Despite their own eternal war against Israeli forces and the world at large, the Arab nations have come up with countless extra weapons for the terrorists in Western Europe. During 1977 and 1979, the Red Brigades made yachting trips to Lebanon for arms, including Skorpions, grenades, machine guns, rockets, and explosives. In Sofia, capital of Red Bulgaria, the PFLP owned a warehouse filled with guns and ammunition, dealing freely with the PLO and IRA, the ETA and Baader-Meinhof gang, the Red Brigades, and Turkish People's Liberation Army. In March 1973, the S.S. *Claudia* was boarded by Irish naval officers, who confiscated five tons of Libyan arms bound for Belfast (including 250 Kalashnikov rifles). Four years later, a search of the S.S. *Towerstream*, off Antwerp, turned up twenty-nine AK 47s, twenty-nine submachine guns, twenty-nine machine pistols, seven rocket launchers, fifty-six rockets, 108 grenades, 428 pounds of TNT, and 400 pounds of plastic explosive — all earmarked for the Provisional IRA.

A surprising source of terrorist supplies throughout the 1970s was Switzerland, where homegrown anarchists grew rich by robbing loosely guarded armories and peddling their loot to friends abroad. In their first three years of operation, the thieves took in 200 rifles, 525 pistols, and 346 grenades for resale to Carlos, the Baader-Meinhofs, and other deserving parties. In 1974 alone, the Swiss "takeout" service stole 123 rifles, 358 pistols, 192 mines, 1,230 pounds of heavy explosives, and 1.5 miles of detonating fuse.

The Anti-Terrorist Response

The worldwide terrorist eruption after 1968 demanded a reaction from the target countries, and while some were slower off the mark than others, every major Western power now maintains a force of antiterrorist commandos in a state of constant readiness against attack. Their history and training methods have been covered in detail by author Bruce Quarrie, in *The World's Elite Forces* (Octopus, 1985), and we have space for only half a dozen nations that have found themselves the special target of concerted terrorist assault.

A pioneering unit in the field of "special operations" is the British Special Air Service (SAS), organized in 1940 to conduct commando raids against the Nazis. Since that time, the SAS has played an active — even vital — role in Malaya, Kenya, Korea, Cyprus, Aden, at Suez, in Muscat and Oman, in Jordan, Kuwait, Belize, and most recently in the Falklands. SAS troops were called to liberate the occupied Iranian embassy in London during May 1980, and their continuing war against the Provisional IRA recently produced controversy with the death of three Irish gunmen at Gibraltar.

Familiar weapons carried by the SAS include the Heckler & Koch MP5 submachine guns (dubbed "Hocklers"), the L42A1 sniper rifle, and the Browning Hi-Power automatic pistol, designated L9A1 by the British. [See Chapter 6.] The unit also uses Britain's standard L1A1 semiautomatic rifle, a modified version of the FAL weapon manufactured by Fabrique Nationale in Belgium. Chambered in 7.62mm, the L1A1 measures 45 inches overall and weighs eleven pounds with loaded 20-round magazine. Modified from the original FAL design at British insistence, it has no capability for full-auto fire.

When members of the SAS aren't packing "Hocklers," chances are they will be carrying the Sterling L2A3 submachine gun or its variant with silencer attached, the L34A1. A modern version of the Sten gun used in World War II, the Sterling resembles its ancestor, with the side-mounted box magazine (on the left), its ventilated barrel shroud, and folding metal stock. Chambered in 9mm Parabellum, the Sterlings measure 19 inches overall with stocks folded, weighing in at 7.65 pounds. Magazines are available with ten or 34 rounds, and the weapon fires at a cyclic rate of 550 rounds per minute.

When heavier weapons are needed for squad support, SAS troops sometimes rely on the L4A4 light machine gun, an updated version of the Bren gun used in World War II. Chambered in 7.62mm, the L4A4 measures 44.6 inches and weighs 21 pounds, mounting a 30-round overhead box magazine. A gas-operated weapon, the Bren fires at a cyclic rate of 500 rounds per minute, hurling projectiles down range at a muzzle velocity of 2,700 feet per second.

Two late additions to the SAS arsenal are the Individual Weapon SL70E3 and its close relative, the Light Support Weapon XL73E2. Basically identical, both guns are chambered in 5.56mm and designed in the "bull-pup" style, with pistol grip and trigger mechanism forward of the 30-round box magazine. Measuring 30.3 inches overall and weighing around 10.14 pounds loaded, the XL weapons average a cyclic fire rate of 700 to 850 rounds per minute, with a muzzle velocity of 2,955 feet per second. Distinguishing features of the Light Support Weapon include a heavier barrel and folding bipod, befitting its intended function as a squad support piece.

From the moment of its birth in 1948, the state of Israel has been constantly at war against the fluctuating forces of the "Palestinian resistance," ranging from a full-scale declaration of hostilities by several nations to the kind of raids where solitary lunatics machine-gun children in their classrooms. Israel has been fighting back (and winning) for the better part of half a century, and it should come as no surprise that her commandos know their job. In case you missed the Six-Day War, recall the great Entebbe raid — dubbed "Operation Thunderbolt" — conducted during June of 1976, with Israeli shock troops liberating hostages from a hijacked airliner in Uganda, 2,000 miles from home.

We covered most of the Israeli standard armament in Chapter 6, including the Beretta 92 series automatics, the Galil Sniping Rifle, and the classic Uzi submachine guns. The Israeli's basic infantry weapon in combat is the Galil ARM assault rifle or its shorter SAR carbine version, chambered in 5.56mm. The ARM measures 38.54 inches overall, with stock folded, and weighs in at 10.19 pounds with a loaded 35-round magazine in place. (Fifty-round magazines are also available.) Firing at a cyclic rate of 650 rounds per minute, the Galil achieves a muzzle velocity of 3,215 feet per second.

Ever since the Sharpeville crisis broke in 1960, the men of the South African Special Services have been fighting a rear-guard action against hopeless odds. Regardless of your politics, the SASS constitutes a major antiterrorist (or counterrevolutionary) group, and it deserves consideration here. Standard equipment for South African commandos includes the Browning Hi-Power automatic, Uzi submachine guns, and the Galil ARM assault rifle, modified with addition of a folding bipod and designated the R4. Specialty numbers include the BXP submachine gun, chambered in 9mm, feeding 22- and 32-round magazines at a cyclic rate of 600 rounds per minute, and the deadly Armsel Striker. The latter is a semiautomatic 12-gauge shotgun, featuring a folding stock and 12-shot rotary magazine. With its forward pistol grip and perforated barrel sleeve, the Striker clearly offered inspiration for the 12-gauge Street Sweeper, now manufactured in America.

Despite her common border with a Russian puppet state, West Germany did not prepare for full-scale antiterrorist activity until Black September gunmen perpetrated their 1972 massacre of athletes at the Olympic games in Munich. Germany's response was the formation of the elite GSG-9 commando unit, which five years later assaulted a hijacked airliner at Mogadishu, in Somalia, killing four terrorists and rescuing ninety hostages. The men of GSG-9 carry Walther PP side arms [Chapter 5] and Uzi submachine guns

[Chapter 6]. They also use the full line of Heckler & Koch weapons, including the MP5 submachine gun, the G3 assault rifle, and the G3 SG/1 sniper's rifle [all discussed in Chapter 6].

Italian forces were dragged into the antiterrorist arena by activities of the Red Brigades, and they have distinguished themselves in recent years with steady gains against the latter. Italian special troops employ the full Beretta line of weapons, including the 92 series automatic pistols and the Model 12 submachine gun [Chapter 6]. Their standard shoulder arm is the Beretta AR70 assault rifle, chambered in 5.56mm. Measuring 37.6 inches overall, the AR70 devours 30-round box magazines at a cyclic rate of 650 rounds per minute, achieving a muzzle velocity of 3,115 feet per second. Numerous accessories include a grenade launcher, bayonet, bipod, telescopic sight, infrared night sights and an optional folding metal stock.

The USA came late to the antiterrorist movement, with creation of the elite Delta Force in November 1977, employing all the standard infantry weapons currently used by American troops, including the Beretta 92F automatic, the M16A1 and CAR 15 assault rifles, Ingram submachine guns, and the army's basic-issue sniper rifles. Delta snipers are required to be a cut above the rest, however, scoring 100 percent hits at 650 yards and 90 percent at 1,100 yards in order to qualify for the unit.

Reading the Riot Act

The modern terrorist in troubled urban areas has various strategic options. He (or she) can use an unrelated violent incident as cover for selected actions, such as ripping off a bank or sniping at police, or he can generate events himself by using trained *provocateurs* to agitate a given neighborhood or stir up violent action on the fringes of a peaceful demonstration. If a clique is large enough — as with the "student groups" in Tokyo and Seoul — it may be possible for terrorists to plan and carry out a riot on their own, allowing unaffiliated citizens to join the action as they please. In any case, control of riot situations is a prime concern in antiterrorist activity, with special weapons and munitions meeting needs of modern law enforcement personnel.

With the exception of regimes that simply open fire on rowdy mobs — as the Algerians were seen to do in October 1988 — most nations try to scatter rioters, disrupting their formations and preventing them from launching mass attacks against police or other targets. Munitions used against a mob may be hand thrown or fired from any one of several launchers, specified below. In general, riot rounds are subdivided into *chemical* and *kinetic* varieties.

Chemical rounds are designed to emit fumes that irritate or disable rioters, with some projectiles containing indelible dye, intended to mark suspects for later arrest. The earliest chemical agent employed against crowds in this century was alpha-chloro-acetophenone, commonly dubbed "tear gas" or CN. Fairly effective in closed spaces, as in flushing a barricaded gunman from cover, CN disperses quickly in the open, minimizing its effect on mobs in riot situations. Rioters have also learned that one gets used to tear gas with prolonged exposure, and a simple handkerchief across the face is often adequate to foil a CN gas attack. A "new" gas, used on crowds beginning in the 1950s, is ortho-chloro-benzalmalono-nitrile, or CS for short. Normally a solid, CS vaporizes on contact with air, producing a gas with the odor of pepper — hence the nickname "pepper gas." CS duplicates the tearing effect of CN, with additional choking and respiratory problems designed to incapacitate humans. In defense against rioters throwing shells back at police, most chemical riot munitions now contain small multiple pellets or canisters, designed to separate and scatter on impact.

Unlike chemical projectiles, the kinetic (or *baton*) rounds are designed to knock selected targets down, presumably without inflicting lethal injury. The early wooden slugs were prone to splinter, causing ugly wounds, and while their rubber replacements will not penetrate human flesh, they can still be lethal at close range. Catholic demonstrators in Northern Ireland have died from the impact of "rubber bullets" to head or chest — the latter causing cardiac arrest in isolated cases — and resultant bad publicity has led to the development of flat-nosed rounds molded from PVC plastic. Lighter than the traditional rubber baton round, PVC projectiles still pack a wallop, but they are less likely to kill their targets.

America, with its long tradition of street demonstrations and social unrest, leads the field in development of riot-control weapons. One popular model is the Smith and Wesson No. 210 Shoulder Gas Gun, chambered in 37mm (1.46 inches), with a maximum range of 150 yards. Measuring 29 inches overall, this single-shot weapon achieves its greatest reach with the No. 14 Goliath projectile, a combination chemical-baton round designed to emit CS gas after penetrating barricades.

Similar in appearance, the single-shot Federal Riot Gun is also chambered in 37mm, with an overall length of 29 inches. Offered with a wide variety of munitions, the weapon achieves its maximum range of 109 yards with the Federal "Speedheat" CS round, engineered to exhaust its gas load within thirty seconds, thus frustrating rioters who try to throw it back. In a similar vein, each Federal SKAT round contains five small CS grenades, designed to bounce through crowds in an erratic, fan-shaped pattern, making retrieval impossible.

Based on a 1930s design, the MM1 Multi-Round Projectile Launcher minimizes the inherent danger of an officer being overrun while reloading his single-shot weapon. Reminiscent of the early Tommy guns or Armsel Striker in appearance, the MM1 features dual pistol grips and a 12-round rotary cylinder. Available in 37mm or 40mm, the MM1 measures 21.5 inches overall, tipping the scales at 19.84 pounds with a full load. The weapon is capable of firing chemical and baton rounds, along with a wide variety of smoke and antipersonnel projectiles, including buckshot, fléchettes, incendiary, and high-explosive rounds. The MM1's design permits a gunner to mix-and-match his ammunition, alternating chemical and kinetic rounds, or mixing explosive, buckshot, and incendiary loads for a more deadly combination.

In riot situations, British soldiers frequently employ the Schermuly Multipurpose Gun, chambered in 37mm, with a maximum range of 164 yards. Using aluminum parts to reduce weight where possible, the Schermuly weighs in at seven pounds, measuring 32.6 inches overall. An alternative weapon, the Arwen, is likewise chambered for 37mm rounds, possessing the benefit of a five-round box magazine. A semiautomatic weapon, weighing 6.83 pounds, the Arwen measures between 29.9 and 33 inches, depending on the extension of its telescoping buttstock. South Africa's Stopper, another single-shot weapon chambered in 37mm, measures 27.56 inches with its stock extended, lobbing heavy baton rounds to a maximum range of 328 yards.

In West Germany, riot troops employ a variation of the standard flamethrower design with their TRGG Portable Irritant Agent Projector. Dual tanks worn on the officer's back contain a pressurized propellant gas (normally carbon dioxide) and the selected irritant (generally CN or CS). Indelible dye can be mixed with the load to mark rioters for later arrest, and empty tanks can be replaced in a matter of seconds, returning the weapon to action. Weighing 45.2 pounds with a full load (23.15 pounds empty), the TRGG has a maximum range of twenty-two yards, with its load equivalent to eighty jets, automatically monitored to reduce waste from gratuitous spraying.

Fire hoses earned a bad rep from "Bull" Connor and his Birmingham police in the 1960s, but a similar principle is still used for crowd control worldwide, in the form of water cannons. Few individuals can stand before a high-pressure stream of water without going down or breaking for cover, and despite propaganda, injuries other than minor bruising (from falls) are virtually unknown. Water cannons have been widely used in Europe and Latin America with excellent results. One model kept on reserve — and thus far unused — in Northern Ireland is dubbed the Special Water Dispenser. Mounted on a British Saracen armored personnel carrier, the SWD is designed to deliver short "slugs" of water — equivalent on impact to the blow from a fist — at ranges up to forty meters. Drawbacks of the water cannon in urban settings include rather limited range (an average thirty meters) and a general inability to overcome sturdy barricades, such as stalled vehicles.

WHODUNIT?

From time to time in fiction, as in life, detectives may be called upon to solve a murder where the cause of death is readily apparent, but the list of suspects, witnesses, and solid evidence is short or even nonexistent. In a shooting case, it may be necessary for the officer to find out where the bullets came from and the type of weapon used. How many shots were fired? Did any miss their target, and if so, where are the bullets now? Does the existing evidence suggest an accidental shooting, suicide, or murder?

Fortunately, many of the questions in an "open" shooting can be answered by examining the bullets, cartridge casings, or the weapon used. An author working in the field of mystery or the police procedural is well advised to check out several textbooks covering the subject of forensic science, but we'll hit the basics here, before we move along.

"Was That a Shot?"

Unless the trigger man is seen by witnesses or captured in the act, police will have to pinpoint his location for themselves. If a murder has been done, the victim won't be going anywhere, and the position of a body may reveal at least the general direction of a bullet's flight. If Victim A is lying face-down on the sidewalk, bags of groceries spilled before him, with a bullet in his back, the chances are that someone shot him from behind, which narrows the field of search to roughly 180 degrees of the compass. Working back along those lines, a search will, hopefully, reveal shell casings, footprints in a flower bed—in short, some solid evidence of where the gunman stood (or parked, or lay in wait).

A bullet hole in any solid, stationary object such as tree trunks, doors, or walls should mark the spent projectile's flight path, leading backward to its point of origin with some degree of accuracy. If there have been several shots, so much the better: through *triangulation* (following the flight paths to their natural conjunction), officers can zero in on a sniper's nest in much the same way monitoring stations trace a radio transmission to its source. A bullet's condition and the depth of penetration may be helpful, also, in determining how far it traveled prior to impact.

An examination of the victim's body may be useful in determining a bullet's flight path, leading backward to the source, but there are also weaknesses in this approach. Extensive tissue damage and the difficulty found in verifying any victim's posture in the final microseconds of his life reduce the likelihood of reconstructing flight paths from the wounds alone. It helps if victims have been shot while sitting in a chair or leaning up against a wall, with bullets passing through to leave a permanent impression, but unfortunately, killers can't be counted on to make things easy for police.

A case in point involves the death of Dr. Martin Luther King in Memphis during April 1968. While he was standing on a balcony of the Lorraine Motel, a single sniper's bullet struck King in the face, shattering on impact, and drove him backward, severing his spine. According to King's autopsy report, "The direction of the wounding was from front to back, above downward, and from right to left." A team of city engineers were sent to clear the matter up—and, incidentally, verify a sniper's nest already singled out by homicide detectives flying in the face of much persuasive evidence—but in the process, they were forced to estimate King's posture, guessing at the angle of his body as he leaned across the railing, calling out to friends below. The end results, "confirmed" by scuff marks in an ancient bathtub and the discovery of "microscopic markings" on a battered windowsill, were adequate to "prove" the shot was fired from a dilapidated rooming house across the street.

Identifying Weapons

Hollywood enjoys an excellent solution rate for homicides, but in real life the numbers leave a lot to be desired. Each year, approximately 25 percent of all domestic murders — some 5,000 cases — go unsolved, and with an average 62 percent of U.S. homicides involving firearms, that means the police have *failed* to identify 3,100 killers and their weapons. Projectile deformity is part of the problem, and even perfect bullets are useless in the absence of a suspect weapon for comparison; but bullets tell us something, all the same.

For openers, a bullet may indicate the caliber of weapon used, provided there's enough to weigh and measure. I say "indicate" instead of "demonstrate" because a bullet starts to change the moment it is fired. Some lose a microscopic portion of themselves before they leave the weapon's barrel, leaving more behind if they are forced to pass through shrubbery, glass, or metal — even fabric — on the way to human flesh. On impact, anything except an armor-piercing round will start to lose its shape immediately as it plows through meat and muscle, body fluids, vital organs. Impact with a bone may stop a bullet cold, divert its course, or smash it into fragments. By the time it comes to rest, it may be scarcely recognizable at all.

(A certain Mississippi sheriff, years ago, presented experts with an object lesson in firearms identification following the murder of a black civil rights worker. Killed by shotgun blasts while driving home one night, the victim had been further injured when his car swerved off the road and struck a tree. Attempting to dismiss the murder as an "accident," the sheriff decided that buckshot pellets taken from the victim's face and neck, were "fillings from his teeth," dislodged on impact with the steering wheel!)

Assuming that a bullet is recovered more or less intact, fired through a rifled barrel, close examination may provide some crucial leads toward pinning down the suspect weapon. During manufacture of the average gun, a rod studded with metal burrs, dubbed the "broach," is drawn through the barrel to produce "rifling." The result is a series of spiral notches, called "grooves," with intervening space between them, known as "lands." Each time a bullet passes through the barrel, it is marked indelibly by lands and grooves, the traces visible beneath a microscope. In turn, the different makes of firearms may be readily identified by counting lands and grooves, determining their width, and studying the barrel's "direction of twist." (A "right-hand" twist indicates clockwise rifling, while "left-hand" twist is counterclockwise.)

An illustrative case is that of California's elusive "Zodiac" killer, still at large a quarter-century after his first known attack. On December 20, 1968, two teenagers were shot and killed while parked on a date at Blue Rock Springs Park near Vallejo, California. No weapon was recovered at the scene, but homicide investigators analyzed the .22-caliber bullets recovered from each victim, counting six right-hand grooves with a land and groove ratio of 1:1 +. In concrete terms, this meant the grooves were .056 inch wide, while the lands measured .060 inch. With these facts in hand, detectives narrowed the field of possible weapons to two suspects: the J.C. Higgins Model 80 or Hi Standard's Model 101. (It hasn't helped, so far, but if they ever find the gun, watch out!)

Spent casings left around a shooting scene are also useful in identifying weapons as to type and make. With bullets in hand, authorities can tell if they are looking for a semiautomatic pistol or revolver, they can verify the caliber or gauge of weapon used, and sometimes even trace the store from which a gunman bought (or stole) his ammunition. Likewise, counting cartridges may help eliminate potential suspect weapons, if their magazine capacity is not sufficient to account for casings found. In yet another double-murder credited to "Zodiac," detectives picked up nine 9mm casings at the scene, immediately ruling out all semiautomatic pistols that could not hold nine or more rounds in their magazines. Likewise, in Chicago, authorities counted casings at the scene of the St. Valentine's Day massacre, concluding that two submachine guns were used, one sporting a 50-round drum, while the other used a 20-round box magazine.

With any luck, specific weapons may be singled out through an examination of their brass and bullets. Cartridge casings left around a shooting scene will bear the microscopic markings from extractor and ejector mechanisms, subject to comparison with any weapons confiscated during the investigation. Likewise, firing pins leave their indelible impression on a cartridge primer—or the rim, in rimfire ammunition—and a microscopic study may reveal if different cartridges were fired and ejected by the same weapon. (Then again, it may not, if the casings have been stepped on, otherwise abused, or if they're left outside to rust and tarnish over time.)

Aside from the impressions left by lands and grooves, which only designate the *type* of weapon used, each bullet carries markings left by tiny imperfections in the barrel. As with human fingerprints and snowflakes, no two weapons leave identical impressions on their bullets, and comparison of suspect bullets with known controls should logically remove all doubt about the "guilt" or "innocence" of a specific weapon. Once again, deformity on impact may prevent comparison, and any extra scratches added in retrieval of the bullet may jeopardize the prosecution's case. Accordingly, physicians must be cautious in removal of a bullet, avoiding further mutilation caused by tongs or forceps. To preserve the chain of evidence, a coroner or surgeon normally inscribes his mark—initials, a case number, whatever—on the nose or base of a bullet, neither of which makes contact with the barrel's interior surface.

Forensic specialists were subject to a lot of eye strain in the early days of firearms testing, scoping in on first one bullet and then another, shifting back and forth, attempting to remember every detail of the first as they examined number two. Their problem was resolved with Dr. Philip Gravelle's invention of the comparison microscope, permitting the simultaneous examination of both bullets. Perfect alignment of markings on two bullets may now be achieved, with photographs of the comparison—called photomicrographs—admissible as evidence in court. (When Fred "Killer" Burke was arrested in April 1930, test rounds from his Tommy gun were positively matched to those retrieved from victims in the St. Valentine's Day Massacre. Though never prosecuted in Chicago, he remains the only gunman positively linked to the event.)

Beating Firearms Identification

Defeating the results of an identification test should be the gunman's third concern, in order of priority. (The first is accuracy; number two is the escape.) If he has left no fingerprints and used a stolen — as opposed to purchased — gun, he may decide to emulate the classic Mafia technique and simply drop his weapon at the scene. A variation on the theme involves disposal of the piece through melt-down, planting in cement, a burial at sea. If, however, your assassin has some kind of personal attachment to his weapon, or he simply can't afford to throw a gun away each time he pulls the trigger, he will have to think about some other ways of foiling his pursuers.

One time-honored method is the use of shotguns to prevent a positive test. A smooth-bore weapon firing clumps of shot, your basic scattergun eliminates the problem of a solitary bullet marked by lands and grooves. If solid bullets are used, the rifling is etched into the lead itself, and will not leave impressions on the barrel. Shotguns have the added benefit of stopping power — one forensics manual describes abdominal wounds as "usually fatal," while head wounds are "always fatal" — and the spray of shot increases the odds of a hit for poor marksmen. These combined attributes have made shotguns a favorite weapon in gang warfare and drive-by shootings from Prohibition-era Chicago to the streets of present-day Los Angeles. (A note of caution here: ejected shotgun shells *will* show the marks of firing pin, extractor, and ejector, so be careful that your gunman doesn't leave his brass behind.)

If shotguns can't be used — your character needs a "silenced" weapon, for example, or concealment is a problem — he may wish to think about replacing barrels after an assassination. We've already mentioned the Dan Wesson line of revolvers [Chapter 6], with their wide variety of barrel lengths and styles, all capable of being changed at home, with simple tools, by any amateur. Most automatic pistols likewise offer easy access to the barrel, once they've been stripped down, and *any* barrel is replaceable if you are willing to invest the time and money in the necessary gear.

Too complicated? Too much work? Then, I'd suggest you have your people take a look at ammunition options in advance, before they get around to pulling triggers. Ammunition should be suited to the situation, always with an eye on its recovery by homicide investigators. Don't call for armor-piercing rounds or big-game rifles if a softer slug or smaller gun will do the job. If bullets are deformed or torn apart on impact, your villain is a long way down the road toward pulling off the perfect crime.

In essence, we're discussing "dum-dum" bullets, now. Designed to flatten or "mushroom" on impact, creating horrific wounds, dum-dums were banned by the Geneva convention in an effort to make global warfare more "humane." They're still around today, in the form of various commercial soft-point and hollow-point ammunition, providing maximum knock-down power in a wide variety of calibers. The rifle used to murder Dr. King in Memphis, Tennessee, has never been reliably identified — and never will — because the killers' choice of ammunition was inspired. Selecting the Remington Soft Point Core-Lokt round, he chose a bullet described by its manufacturer as "the No. 1 mushroom," specifically designed to double its caliber on impact. The resultant distortion obliterates land and groove markings, along with any other distinctive characteristics of the projectile.

If commercial dum-dum rounds are unavailable, a competent assassin can produce his own by drilling out a bullet's tip or otherwise mutilating the projectile in advance of firing. Hand-loading of cartridges permits a gunman to play around with both propellant charges — reducing a load to increase the efficiency of "silenced" weapons — and projectiles. Bullets with a hollow base may be inverted in the loading process, so the open "cone" becomes the bullet's nose. If you are trying to imagine the result, picture a Dixie cup being crushed against someone's forehead — with a sledgehammer.

In addition to dum-dums, handguns of all calibers will also accommodate shot shells. Designed for hunting and defense against snakes in the wild, these rounds turn your pistol into a mini-shotgun, and most of them have lethal potential at close range. The modern antipersonnel version is a lethal number called the Glaser Safety Slug, sporting pellets of shot suspended in liquid teflon, for detonation on impact. Glasers are "safe" because they will not ricochet or drill through doors and walls, but it's another story for a man on the receiving end. At last report, in 1981, Glasers had been fired at ninety men by law enforcement personnel. All ninety had been one-shot stops, with eighty-nine immediate DOAs and one survivor — the latter a particular surprise, since liquid teflon in the bloodstream generally produces heart failure.

A word in passing on the freak loads — bullets made from wood, glass, ice, whatever. If you're bent on traveling along these lines, by all means, by my guest. But you should be aware that freak loads are inherently unstable, short on range and accuracy, long on risks of failure. Some may shatter on firing; others may be so distorted or ungainly that they never even reach the target. It's intriguing to consider bullets made of ice, designed to melt inside a wound, but bear in mind that they will start to melt the moment they are taken from the freezer and inserted into a gun. Ten minutes or an hour later, with his bullets turned to water and the powder in his cartridges reduced to sodden paste, your super-villain will be helpless and unarmed.

We've seen that empty casings can identify a murder weapon, and a savvy killer will attempt to minimize the clues he leaves behind. One option is avoidance of the semiautomatic weapons, sticking with revolvers if a silencer is not required for the specific job. Various single-shot and double-barreled weapons are also available, retaining spent cases until the action is "broken" for reloading. Manually operated weapons of the lever-, slide-, and bolt-action varieties likewise keep their brass to themselves, as long as you can do your killing with a single shot.

If there are several targets, or your gunman is committed to a semiautomatic weapon for whatever reason, there are going to be cartridges ejected at the scene. With time to spare — a murder in an isolated setting, for example — he may wish to stop and pick them up before he leaves. Assuming he can find them all. A better, quicker method is the use of a "brass-catcher," commonly used by sportsmen who save their used brass for reloading. Available to anyone, including sales by mail-order, brass catchers are manufactured to fit most semiautomatic weapons, while custom jobs may be obtained from any competent gunsmith.

Matching Man and Gun

With the exception of clandestine items — whipped up for assassins, secret agents, and the like — and homemade "zip guns," every firearm manufactured in the Western world bears a unique serial number, recorded by its maker, logged in commercial records at each point of transfer through licensed hands. Thus, a weapon discarded at a California murder scene may be easily traced to its point of sale in a Texas gun shop, and on from there to its origins in a Connecticut factory. The chain may be broken in various ways, via theft or a transfer between private parties, but at least there is some starting point for an investigation. If pistol number 1234567 was manufactured last year in New York, sold to John Doe in Los Angeles a month later, and found at the scene of a bank robbery yesterday, police begin their investigation by grilling Mr. Doe. It may turn out that the gun was stolen, sold, or traded to another owner shortly after purchase, passing through a dozen different hands before it wound up in that bank, but any lead is better than a yawning void.

Sometimes, a weapon's I.D. number may embarrass the authorities by shooting holes in their solution of a case. When "public enemy" John Dillinger was killed by G-men in Chicago, in July of 1934, it was reported that the agents found a pistol in his pocket. The weapon — a Colt .38-caliber automatic bearing serial number 119702 — has been on display at FBI headquarters ever since, a trophy of the hunt, but modern research indicates the outlaw may, in fact, have been unarmed when he was shot. Checking the Colt's serial number through factory records, author Jay Robert Nash discovered that Colt #119702 was delivered to the L.H. Kurz Company, in Des Moines, Iowa, on December 19, 1934 — a full five months after Dillinger's death in Chicago! Likewise, when Robert Kennedy was gunned down in Los Angeles in 1968, police reported a positive match between the fatal bullets and test rounds fired through Sirhan B. Sirhan's revolver. Unfortunately, Sirhan's weapon bore serial number H53725, while LAPD reports indicate the "positive match" was achieved with test bullets fired from a different revolver, bearing serial number H18602.

Back in the good old days, when any klutz could plunk down his money and purchase a Tommy gun over the counter, gangsters realized the necessity of eliminating serial numbers. Files were used initially, grinding the numerals out of existence, but applications of acid restored the incriminating numbers to legibility. Soon, criminals began gouging deeper with various chisels and drills, weeding out any trace of the manufacturer's mark. Their task is made more difficult today by the stamping of multiple brands on each weapon, tucking serial numbers away in various nooks and crannies. Removal or alteration of firearms serial numbers is also a crime in itself, regardless of the perpetrator's intent.

In spite of Hollywood's pronouncements to the contrary, firearms rank among the worst potential sources for latent finger-prints. Most handguns have some sort of textured or checkered grip plates, while many have grooves on the backstrap, trigger, and hammer. None of these rough surfaces will hold a fingerprint or palmprint, and the weapon itself is frequently coated in oil or pow-der residue from recent firing. Still, a wary gunman won't leave anything to chance, since even one clear print may be enough to land him on death row.

Avoiding fingerprints — on guns or any other object — takes some thought and foresight. I'm aware of some professionals who coat their fingertips with glue, in preference to wearing gloves, but palmprints are admissible in court, and gloves are still the safest way to go, all things considered. If your character is wiping down a weapon to eliminate the prints, he should wipe *everything* (includ-ing cartridges, *before* they're loaded in the gun). When JFK was shot in Dallas, local officers reported finding no prints on a rifle picked up in the Texas Book Depository. Experts at the FBI lab found a perfect palmprint underneath the barrel, hidden by the forestock when the weapon was assembled. Phrased another way, forgetfulness can get you fried.

The discharge of a weapon automatically releases gas and powder residue, with particles containing nitrates in suspension that adhere to any human flesh in contact with the gun.

The standard test used now (taking the place of the former paraffin test) is to use swabs moistened with dilute nitric acid. The swab can then be examined by neutron activation analysis (NAA); atomic absorption (AA), or scanning electron microscopy (S&M). Flashing back again to Dallas, paraffin tests performed on Lee Harvey Oswald revealed nitrates on both hands but none on his face, suggesting that (a) he found a new way of aiming his rifle, (b) he somehow washed his face without cleaning his hands at the same time, or (c) he may not have fired the rifle at all.

If casings are recovered at a crime scene, and cartridges of the same brand are later found in a suspect's possession, the coinci-dence may be suggestive of guilt, but with millions of rounds manu-factured each year, a more positive test is required. One such tech-nique is spectrographic analysis, in which a test substance is deliberately irradiated, causing each component element to emit a distinct spectrum of light. These spectra are recorded on film, analyzed both qualitatively (to learn which elements are present) and quantitatively (to determine the relative percentage of each in the sample). Through spectrographic analysis and neutron activation analysis — an even more sensitive test, capable of naming component elements to the millionth of a part — specific rounds may be compared to unfired bullets from a suspect batch, with some remarkable results.

In one recorded case, a man escaped conviction when analysis of bullets extracted from a wounded victim turned up traces of antimony, but none of tin. A box of ammunition confiscated from the suspect's home revealed antimony, as well, but there were also microscopic particles of tin in each and every bullet tested from the box, a fact that sank the prosecution's case. In another instance, a night watchman opened fire on burglars who escaped, leaving traces of blood at the scene. An injured suspect, picked up by police, refused to give an explanation for his wounds, but spectrographic analysis revealed that bullet fragments extracted from his leg had not been fired through the watchman's revolver. Likewise, in a third case where the human target was spared by a bullet striking his cigarette case, spectrographic analysis of sample rounds cleared the prime suspect of any involvement in the shooting.

Who Shot Whom?

In the course of a day's work, homicide detectives and forensics experts may be called upon to determine whether a shooting was accidental or deliberate, a suicide, or murder. Close examination of the body should provide some crucial answers in regard to angle and position of the weapon, distance from the point of impact, and the power of its load. A close-range shot, as in most suicides, will mark the victim's flesh with powder flash-burns and "tattoos" — that is, with particles of powder penetrating the skin. If a victim's arms are twenty-seven inches long, it should be obvious he did not hold a pistol six feet from his head to make a killing shot. (Likewise, in a suicide by shotgun or rifle, the victim will have to reach the trigger with fingers — or toes — in order to succeed.)

The angle and position of a fatal shot may also indicate that homicide has been committed. Victims clearly cannot shoot themselves in the back, for example, and the accidental discharge of a firearm will rarely result in descending flight paths. There are also certain probabilities involved, with the majority of gunshot suicides involving head wounds. Individuals rarely shoot themselves any-where else, although it has happened. In 1965, humiliated by expo-sure of his Jewish background, Klan leader Dan Burros opted to expunge his "shame" through suicide. The project was accom-plished when he shot himself twice in the chest.

America averages some 2,000 accidental firearms deaths per year, with careless hunters and children accounting for most of the casualties, but sensible adults also manage to shoot themselves from time to time. (Most of the police officers killed in ghetto riots during the 1960s were, in fact, cut down by "friendly fire.") A rifle or a shotgun, standing with a live round in the chamber, may be lethal if it falls, but modern handguns are surprisingly immune to accidental discharge, if they're handled with a modicum of com-mon sense and caution.

"Automatic" pistols are the safest of the lot, on balance, with the vast majority employing several safety mechanisms. In addition to the classic safety lever, which prevents trigger-pull, other com-mon systems include magazine and grip safeties. The former pre-vents a weapon from firing under any circumstances once the mag-azine has been removed, even if a round has been forgotten in the chamber. Grip safeties, on the other hand, incorporate a "dead man's switch," requiring pressure from a normal grip to free the piece for firing. Used on Uzis, Llama automatics, the classic Colt .45s and other semiauto arms, grip safeties prevent a dropped weapon from discharging, even when it is cocked with a live round in the firing chamber. In the case of double-action automatics, carried with a round inside the chamber and the hammer down, deliberate trigger-pull is required to fire the first shot.

Revolvers have no safety switch, per se, but that does not mean they are prone to accidental firing. Whether single- or dou-ble-action, high-quality arms such as Colts, Smith and Wessons, Dan Wessons, and Rugers all incorporate some mechanism that blocks the firing pin until the trigger is pulled. You can drop a quality revolver on the floor or hit the hammer with a tire iron, and the piece will not go off, unless it has been cocked or the internal mechanism tampered with in some respect.

Admittedly, we've only scratched the surface of forensics

here, and authors who intend to make a mint with mysteries or hot police procedurals should take the time for in-depth research on firearms identification techniques and related subjects. Relevant material is available from most large libraries, while periodicals aimed at a police market offer many such textbooks for mail-order sale.

T E N
SPORTING ARMS

Barring access to police or military arsenals, a weapons factory, or secret stockpiles kept on hand by some extremist group, your characters will have to put their trust in everyday civilian pieces, also known as "sporting" arms. The "sports" involved are basically divided into target shooting (everything from tin-can "plinking" to the medal round of the Olympic games) and hunting (anything from squirrels and "varmints" to the disappearing game of Africa). Such weapons come in every caliber and price range, from inexpensive "youth" models to match rifles and professional skeet guns costing thousands of dollars each.

American shooters take their sport seriously, laying out millions each year for firearms, ammunition, and the related expenses of camping equipment, hunting licenses, targets, camouflage clothing, range fees—you name it. Along the way, they have developed a bewildering variety of calibers and weapons, most of which we won't have time or space to itemize, but I intend to hit the major types and say a word or two about their functions. If you're into lists and illustrations, I suggest you find the latest volume of the *Shooter's Bible*, published annually in paperback, and check out everything from barrel lengths and weight to the selected retail price on any weapon of your choice.

Sporting Rifles

We've already covered military rifles, and a number of civilian models that are often drafted into service by police departments, but we've barely scratched the surface up to now. Americans are free to choose from foreign and domestic models, in a wide variety of calibers and styles. We've come a long way from the muzzle-loading musket (though they're still around, as we shall see), and rifles have become sophisticated to the point that one is probably available for any job you have in mind. The modern range includes both centerfire and rimfire weapons, offered in no less than half a dozen basic styles.

Least popular among the modern offerings are single-shot rifles, including two distinct types: some are classic singles, patterned on the weapons of the wild frontier, while others are simply single-shot versions of modern bolt-action magazine rifles. Centerfire singles evolved from the early Sharps and Remington models, falling into disrepute with hunters who sought larger ammo capacities in the 1920s and the early 1930s. The latter Thirties witnessed the arrival of assorted "varmint" cartridges for medium- and long-range work, including the .218 Bee, .219 Zipper, .22 Hornet, .220 Swift, and the .257 Roberts. By the 1950s, gunsmith Wilbur Hauck was turning out a few single-shots of his own design, but the true revival began in 1967, with the introduction of Ruger's Number One model. Modern centerfire singles include rifles from Ruger and Browning, together with some frontier replicas like the Harrington & Richardson Springfields.

Modern rimfire ammunition is all .22-caliber, available in Short, Long, and Long Rifle varieties. As variants of the modern bolt-action rifles, .22 singles will chamber all three types of ammunition. Cost-wise, it is all or nothing with these weapons, as they break down into basic "youth" models or match-quality rifles selling for hundreds of dollars. Unlike bolt-action repeaters, most rimfire singles must be manually cocked after a round is chambered, making them fairly safe weapons in sensible hands.

Lever-action rifles date back to the Volcanic and Henry models, owing much of their modern appearance to the classic frontier Winchesters. Despite occasional experiments with rotary and box magazines, most centerfire lever-actions use a tubular magazine mounted under the barrel. They are available with exposed hammers and in "hammerless" models, ejecting spent casings either through the top of the receiver (in Winchesters) or out the side (in Marlins, the M99 Savage, and others). Top-ejection models can be tricky for a marksman who is interested in telescopic sights, requiring that a scope be offset or mounted forward of the receiver, but Winchester fans don't seem to mind. Lever-action rimfires made their debut in 1873, as the oldest rimfire magazine rifles, and they're still with us today. All modern versions feature external hammers and tubular magazines mounted below the barrel.

We've already covered bolt-action centerfire magazine rifles in their military/police applications [Chapter 6], and the same weapons are widely used by hunters. Single-shot centerfire bolt-action guns are the most limited category of rifles, restricted to use in hunting "varmints" (coyotes and assorted smaller animals), match shooting (including international competition), and bench-rest work. The latter sport consists entirely of a shooter trying to put three rounds through the same hole at long range. Bench-rest weapons are classified by weight: weapons in the sporting rifle class weigh 8.5 pounds or less with scope attached; varmint rifles, with scope, weigh a maximum of 11.5 pounds; while weapons in the "any-weight" class are sometimes found to exceed 40 pounds. The bolt-action rimfire repeater was a late starter, making its first appearance in 1922. Today, such weapons are available with tubular or detachable in-line box magazines.

Slide-action rifles—often called "pump" or "trombone" models—are the fastest of the manually operated actions, approaching the speed of semiautomatic weapons in competent hands. Centerfire models are available with tubular or detachable box magazines from Remington and Savage, with one such—the Remington M760 Gamemaster—gaining notoriety for its alleged role in the King assassination. Slide-action rimfires are found in both "hammerless" and exposed-hammer versions, but all utilize tubular magazines, mounted underneath the barrel.

After decades of experimentation with long and short recoil, modern semiautomatic rifles chambered for centerfire cartridges all use the gas-operated action with side ejection. Most utilize a detachable box magazine, but the Ruger M44 carbine — chambered in .44 Magnum — uses a tubular magazine in its forend. Semiauto rimfires, introduced by Winchester in 1904, are today the best-selling .22-caliber rifles around. Cartridge size and power limits semiauto rimfires to the blowback method, with no recorded complaints from their users. Various models incorporate detachable in-line box magazines or tubular mags, variously mounted in the buttstock, underneath the barrel, or inside the forend.

Double-barreled rifles are restricted to the big-game field, safari style, and none are presently available in rimfire. Normally manufactured in Britain, double-barrels are characterized by large bores and brutal recoil, punishing the elephant or rhino hunter with a kick that has been known to spin a light-weight man around or knock him off his feet. These rare, expensive weapons may be found in side-by-side or over/under formats, variously sporting single or double triggers.

Sporting Shotguns

Modern shotguns are a bit more limited than rifles. None are presently available in rimfire, and there are no lever-action models, but they otherwise compete in terms of different actions, size, and function. Starting with the biggie, shotguns are available in 10-, 12-, 20-, 28-, and .410-gauge (the latter something of a renegade, as it is really measured out in hundredths of an inch, like caliber). Commercial ammunition offers several types of birdshot, buckshot, and the heavy rifled slugs presumably reserved for deer or larger game. More commonly employed for home defense than rifles, shotguns offer stopping power and increase the odds of mediocre marksmen scoring hits within the limits of a gun's effective range.

Single-shot pieces are rather sharply divided between the inexpensive models, favored by children or economy-minded farm types, and professional trap guns, which may cost $5,000 or more in custom editions. Either way, the chief drawback with single-shot weapons is simply the fact that they *are* single-shots. You may inject suspense into a scene by having a hunter or homeowner stalked by several adversaries, wondering whether he can reload fast enough to stay alive in a killing situation, but your average hit-man wouldn't touch the singles with a ten-foot pole. The weapons are employed by many street gangs, junkies, and the like, because of their simplicity and cost (no charge, if stolen from your local sporting goods emporium). A single-shot with butt and barrel trimmed away can make a lethal close-range "pistol," and they do a decent job on single-target drive-by shootings, too.

As in the case of rifles, double-barreled shotguns may be found in either side-by-side or over/under variations, sporting single or double triggers. Over/unders are the most popular multishot nonrepeating weapons on the market today, with various models employed for both hunting and trap shooting. It is not uncommon to find over/under shotguns chambered in two different gauges — .410 over .20-gauge, for example — and some manufacturers even turn out rifle-shotgun combinations, usually with the single-shot rifle barrel on top. The Germans, who have made most of these, also have the rifle barrel on the bottom.

Side-by-side doubles, once the classic shotgun of the West, fell out of favor with Americans in the two decades after World War II. They enjoyed a modest comeback in the 1960s, with certain defense-minded shooters appreciating the side-by-side's intimidating appearance. Commonly used for both hunting and trap shooting, the side-by-side doubles are available with single or double triggers. With the exception of some Wild West replicas (manufactured in Italy!), none of the modern double-barrels feature the classic exposed hammers.

We've already discussed the military/police applications of slide-action shotguns [Chapters 4 and 6], but we could stand a word or two about their sporting applications. Used for both hunting and trap shooting, modern "pump" guns universally feature internal hammers, introduced by John Browning in 1903. Some of the older exposed-hammer Winchester types are still around, but they are bona fide antiques and no such weapons are produced today. American game laws restrict shotguns to a maximum load of three rounds, and manufacturers comply with this regulation by inserting a "plug" — usually a piece of wooden dowling — in the magazine before a gun is boxed for shipment. It is relatively simple to remove the plug and thus expand a magazine's capacity, while special magazine extensions are available, accommodating up to ten rounds, based upon the barrel's length. Except for Ithacas in 12- and 20-gauge, slide-action shotguns normally eject spent casings from the right-hand side of the receiver.

Prior to 1939, most semiautomatic shotguns operated on the long recoil system, but only the Browning Auto 5 still uses the method today. Gas-operated weapons dominate the current field of self-loaders, with casings universally ejected from the right-hand side of the receiver. (An exception proves the rule: some left-hand custom models are available, if shooters wish to pay the extra price.) Semiauto shotguns will normally come with the same magazine plugs used in slide-action repeaters, and removal is no more complex.

The one and only bolt-action shotgun available from domestic sources is the Marlin Model 55 "goose gun," designed for killing migratory waterfowl at high altitudes. Tipping the scale at eight pounds with its two-round clip magazine loaded, the goose gun features a 36-inch full-choked barrel for maximum range.

Handguns

While modern pistols are undoubtedly procured most often as a means of self-defense (or criminal assault), some also lend themselves to the classic sporting pursuits of hunting and target shooting. Indeed, while some handguns are clearly designed as man-stoppers, others have no apparent function beyond the punching of targets. There's something for everyone in the wide world of pistols, and space limitations prevent us from taking more than a quick glance at the major varieties.

For obvious reasons, the popularity of single-shot handguns has plummeted since the nineteenth-century introduction of successful revolvers. A poor choice for self-defense, used sporadically by dedicated one-shot hunters, most centerfire singles are designed for target work. (One exception, American Derringer's single-shot .38 Special, is designed as a hideout piece, for killing at close range.) Remington's XP-100 is a bolt-action piece, chambered for the .221 Remington Fireball cartridge, while the break-top Thompson/Center Contenders will accommodate more than a dozen calibers, including some full-size rifle cartridges. Single-shot rimfires are the narrowest of all handgun categories, with the limited offerings strictly intended for target practice.

Multibarreled pistols were popular during the nineteenth century, but few remain on the market today. American Derringer offers three models, ranging from 4.82 inches to 8.2 inches in overall length, available in both .22-caliber rimfire and various centerfire calibers. The four-barreled Model 422, from Advantage Arms, is chambered in .22 caliber, with an option for .22 Magnum. Advertised as "the world's safest handgun," the Model 422 features an internal hammer, a double-action trigger requiring adult finger pressure, and a rotating firing pin recessed away from the cartridges. Presumably designed as a hideout or back-up weapon, the 2.5-inch barrel rules out any serious hunting or target applications.

No longer employed as military/police weapons, single-action revolvers remain popular as nostalgia pieces, utilized for hunting, target work, and occasional fast-draw competitions (normally using blank ammunition). Six-shot replicas of favorite frontier models are available from Colt, Dakota, Interarms, and Navy Arms, while single-action Rugers merge the "cowboy" look with modern magnum calibers. Various rimfire replicas are also available, used primarily for "plinking" and other forms of inanimate target practice.

We dealt with double-action centerfire revolvers back in Chapters 4 and 6, but there are also sporting applications of the weapons favored by American police. Heavy "bull barrels" are frequently attached to revolvers for target work, thereby reducing recoil, and magnum calibers are frequently fitted with scopes to serve as hunting weapons, capable of dropping bear and other large game. Rimfire wheelguns are scaled-down copies of the larger double-action arms, but unlike single-action rimfires, some double-action .22s carry eight or nine rounds in their cylinders. (One such, an inexpensive Harrington & Richardson piece, was allegedly used to assassinate Robert Kennedy in June 1968. Police are still trying to explain how Sirhan's eight-shot weapon could account for thirteen to fifteen bullet holes in flesh, walls, door jambs and ceiling panels.)

As discussed in Chapters 4 through 7, centerfire semiautomatic pistols are primarily designed for military/police and self-defense applications. Rimfire "automatics," introduced by John Browning in 1913, are usually employed for plinking, target matches, or small-game hunting, but self-defense applications are not unknown. Bersa .22-caliber pistols, the Charter Arms Model

40, the F.I.E. Titan II, Iver Johnson's TP22, and the Beretta small frame automatics are all clearly designed as antipersonnel arms, their short barrels rendering target work or serious hunting impractical.

Paramilitary Arms

For those who find the range of sporting arms inadequate, civilian buyers also have their choice of paramilitary weapons, modified to fire in semiautomatic with assorted alterations to the barrels, magazines, and firing mechanisms. Semiautomatic "carbine" versions of the Tommy gun and Uzi submachine gun are available with 16-inch barrels, while shorter "pistol" variants of each — minus buttstocks — are also offered for sale. Semiauto versions of the Ingram submachine gun are likewise advertised as pistols for civilian customers, and assault rifles have not been neglected, either. A cash outlay of $300 to $1,200 will deliver semiautomatic versions of the Armalite, Beretta, Colt, Fabrique Nationale, Galil, Heckler & Koch, Kalashnikov, or Steyr AUG rifles on demand, including various models chambered for .22-caliber rimfire and 9mm Parabellum cartridges. Even the Barrett Light Fifty sniper's rifle is available over the counter, priced in the neighborhood of $3,500.

Many of the "special" arms on sale today are military surplus or replicas of same. Iver Johnson manufactures copies of the M1 carbine for civilian buyers, with a sawed-off "pistol" version known as the Enforcer. Springfield Armory produces replicas of the venerable M1 Garand, along with a semiauto M14 Clone dubbed the M1A Standard Model. Foreign import deals have also dumped large numbers of Italian, Chinese, German, British, Spanish, and Egyptian weapons on the U.S. market, with increasing numbers of Eastern Bloc rifles from Yugoslavia, Czechoslovakia, and the USSR.

Black Powder Arms

For the ultimate in nostalgia, at least thirteen American firms produce black powder muskets, rifles, shotguns, and pistols, including flintlock and percussion designs. Occasionally used for hunting, black powder arms turn up more frequently at pioneer celebrations, traditional turkey shoots, and in the hands of Civil War reenactment groups. Many of these weapons are traditional muzzle-loaders, complete with all the original drawbacks of slow reloading, inconvenient ammunition, and tell-tale clouds of smoke produced with every shot. (On the other side of the coin, as certified "antiques," the sale of black powder arms is generally not regulated under current firearms legislation.) I won't fault anyone who has the inclination, ready cash, and time to dress like Davy Crockett, creeping through the woods in search of some adventure, but if you're considering black powder as a modern form of self-defense, you ought to have your head examined.

"There Oughta Be a Law"

In fact, there is. Two centuries have passed since our enlightened founding fathers stuck a gun amendment in the Bill of Rights, and firearms regulations have been raising hackles ever since, with certain factions working overtime to limit ownership, the opposition fighting tooth and nail against restrictions. I am not about to enter the morass of "gun control" debates, but authors should be conscious of existing legislation when they set about to arm their characters in fiction. Readers may begin to doubt your expertise — perchance your sanity — if characters are seen to purchase pistols in a city where their sale is banned, procure machine guns at their local sporting goods emporium, or carry weapons on a plane without a second thought to modern-day security procedures.

Your safest guide to local firearms regulations would be law enforcement or a licensed dealer. A compendium of state and local laws is published by the IRS Bureau of Alcohol, Tobacco, and Firearms (BATF), with copies distributed to most firearms dealers and some libraries. Likewise, most larger libraries will possess copies of their state's criminal code, with firearms rules and regulations clearly indexed for convenience. It would take another volume twice this size to itemize the gun laws passed in fifty states, and since we don't have time or space, let's focus on a few of the preeminent examples.

Following the Prohibition wars and "Kansas City Massacre," Congress was moved to produce the National Firearms Act of 1934, restricting ownership of so-called gangster weapons. Covering machine guns, silencers, and sawed-off firearms — that is, shotguns with a barrel under 18 inches long, or rifles with a barrel under 16 inches — this bill didn't outlaw anything, per se. Instead, it set up roadblocks to the ownership of the enumerated weapons, requiring registration with the Treasury Department and payment of a $200 transfer tax each time a regulated item changes hands. The several states were left at liberty to pass more stringent legislation on their own, and while some states (like California and New York) have made it more or less impossible to buy an automatic weapon, others have seen fit to let the feds take care of any problems by themselves. By raising prices and requiring federal registration, Congress managed to retard the sale of what are known as Class III weapons, but their sale was not specifically prohibited, as such.

It takes a rash of violence to produce new firearms legislation, and the 1960s fit the bill, with various assassinations raising cries for a domestic weapons freeze. The National Firearms Act of 1968 banned mail order shipment of guns or ammunition (except between licensed dealers), placed new restrictions on interstate transportation or sale of firearms, mandated a minimum age of twenty-one years for the purchase of handguns, and whipped up a whole new list of restricted "destructive devices," including all manner of artillery, rocket launchers, flamethrowers, grenades, and sundry other items overlooked in 1934. Unless one of your characters is a gun dealer — or you've set your story prior to '68 — the free-wheeling purchase of guns by mail or in neighboring states is a definite no-no.

One of our most recent federal firearms laws, passed in 1987, came as a response to the complaints of paramilitary weapons being used against police by criminal assailants. Under this law, no full-automatic weapons manufactured since the spring of 1987 may be sold to — or possessed by — a civilian shooter. Weapons of an older vintage, manufactured prior to passage of the law, are still accessible to any buyer with the cash on hand, provided he or she conforms to local, state, and federal law in all respects.

Where local legislation now exists, it normally bans ownership of firearms by mental patients and convicted felons, restricts the public carrying of concealed weapons, and requires those weapons carried openly to be unloaded inside city limits. Many jurisdictions presently require a "cooling-off" period between the purchase and delivery of a handgun, with the delay ranging from two or three days to a period of weeks. (No such restrictions presently apply to rifles or shotguns.) Some metropolitan areas—like Las Vegas— permit open sale of pistols but require their subsequent registration with police; others—like New York City— require special permits for handgun ownership. (New York's famous Sullivan Law has been on the books for six decades, without putting an appreciable dent in local mayhem.) A handful of communities have seen fit to ban pistols completely, while at least one *requires* every adult male to own a weapon.

Where the local laws restrict the ownership of firearms, you can count on black-market weapons filling the gap. Prohibition of any item instantly hikes the price, and a revolver selling legally for $200 in Iowa may command two or three times the money from Manhattan street dealers. In Japan, where firearms are essentially banned, modest Smith & Wesson revolvers may command a black-market price of $2,500 each, with ammunition selling briskly at a rate of five to twelve dollars *per bullet*.

GROUND ZERO

We've saved the best for last, to close out with a bang. Explosives are not firearms, granted, but the topics — and the hardware — have a natural affinity for one another, dating back to the Chinese invention of gunpowder and Alfred Nobel's much later creation of dynamite. In military combat situations, terrorist activities and the police response to same, and in many "normal" crimes, explosive charges play a crucial role. If your protagonists or heavies plan on blowing someone up, you're well advised to learn a bit about the subject in advance.

The Sources of Explosives

Problems of supply will not exist if you are dealing with police or military characters, but otherwise you'll have to think about the question of supply before your characters start to plant their charges. It is possible to purchase various explosives on the "open" market, but remember that possession is restricted by innumerable local, state, and federal laws. If nothing else, the buyer will be forced to show I.D. and sign for any purchase; more than likely, there will also be a series of permits and licenses required before he takes delivery. Too much? Too slow? In that case, your characters will be forced to fall back on one of the three illicit sources for explosives.

We discussed established terrorist suppliers back in Chapter 8, and you should note that certain countries in the Middle East, as well as nations of the Eastern Bloc, both manufacture and distribute various explosives to their customers around the world. Those customers include a host of terrorists and self-styled revolutionaries, armed by Mother Russia—or the Libyans, the Saudis, the Chinese, the Czechs—with everything from hand grenades to TNT and guided missiles. On a smaller scale, in the United States, the FBI and BATF agents spent a large part of the 1960s tracking licensed firearms and explosives dealers who were trading secretly with members of the Ku Klux Klan, the Minutemen, and other right-wing paramilitary groups. In some cases the dealers *were* members, donating weapons, ammunition, and explosives to the "cause" at cost, or even free of charge.

If any group or individual can't buy munitions, theft becomes a logical alternative. American outlaws have been raiding police stations and National Guard armories since the 1930s, at least, and we've already seen [Chapter 8] how Swiss anarchists supplied themselves and their friends through the 1970s with theft from military stores. In February 1975, the so-called New World Liberation Front stole various explosives from a quarry at Fenton, California, using their loot to manufacture at least nine bombs, which were planted or mailed throughout the state. In Dixie, members of the Klan are known to steal dynamite from blasting sites whenever possible, with members on the building crews removing a few sticks each night, in their lunch pails. Between 1965 and 1967, members of the ultrasecret "Silver Dollar" group used stolen TNT in its campaign against blacks in Mississippi and Louisiana, killing one victim and crippling another for life.

In 1971, raiders from the Baader-Meinhof gang stole a shipment of hand grenades from the U.S. Army base at Miesau, West Germany, afterward passing them out to allied terrorists around

Europe. Several were used by members of the Japanese Red Army, when they occupied the French embassy at the Hague on September 13, 1974, demanding — and securing — the release of their monetary bag man, Yoshiaka Yamada. Two days later, in Paris, Carlos the Jackal "supported" Japanese demands by hurling another stolen grenade into Le Drugstore, killing two persons and wounding another dozen. More grenades from the same stolen shipment were also used by Carlos and his gang when they invaded OPEC headquarters at Vienna, in December 1975.

Britain's minuscule Angry Brigade showed a preference for explosives stolen in France, smuggling supplies of Gomme L, Nitromite, and Nitrotex into the country from sources abroad. Authorities had no sure way of tracing an explosive to its source, beyond a fruitless visit to the manufacturer, but lately the security police in Britain and Ireland have developed various new techniques. One such involves the insertion of colored threads or various chemical compounds into commercial explosives during production, marking their intended point of sale or distribution for the record. When recognized threads or chemical traces are identified after a blast, authorities may now determine where the prime ingredients were bought — or stolen — by the bombers.

When all other avenues fail, bombers can still manufacture their own explosives, with some impressive results. We're not conducting a crash course in chemistry here, but if you're interested in recipes, check out your local bookstore or write away for the catalogs of several "survivalist" publishing houses. You may not find that American Nazi Party classic, *Explosives Like Grandpa Used to Make*, but you can probably get your hands on *The Anarchist's Cookbook* or *The Poor Man's James Bond*.

You are surrounded every day by chemicals that can be mixed with startling results. The IRA produces many of its explosive charges from a mixture of common garden chemicals and diesel fuel, available to anyone with ready cash in hand. In August 1970, a bomb whipped up from fuel oil and nitrogen fertilizer leveled a research laboratory at the University of Wisconsin, killing a graduate student. Karleton Armstrong, who had purchased the ingredients, spent some time on the FBI's "Ten Most Wanted" list before he was finally picked up and jailed on charges of second-degree murder. The prime disadvantage of "fertilizer bombs" lies in sluggish ignition, normally requiring a primer charge like gun cotton to detonate the main charge. Advantages include the ready availability of ingredients and simplicity of transportation in bulk, making the charges ideal for use in car bombs.

In the early 1960s, members of the Ku Klux Klan and various related groups organized a secret clique called Nacirema — that's "American," spelled backwards — to conduct a string of demolition seminars. They used to bring their families along, the wives and children fixing lunch while Klansmen practiced blasting stumps and wiring dynamite beneath the hoods of junk cars brought along for the occasion. One of Nacirema's specialties was homemade napalm, whipped up from a blend of gasoline and laundry soap, designed to give the standard Molotov cocktail more staying power. Sealed in a Mason jar, with a firecracker or cherry bomb for ignition, the recipe was ideal for torching homes and churches — or for gutting a carload of civil rights workers on some lonely Southern highway.

Fuses

Once a bomber has obtained ingredients and manufactured his explosive package, he will need a way to set it off. With highly sensitive explosives — such as nitroglycerine — a simple jolt may be enough to do the job, but most explosives need a fuse and primer charge to get things rolling. Sure, I know you've seen a hundred movies where a charge of dynamite is detonated by the impact of a bullet, but remember, that was Hollywood, the land of perfect silencers and guns that never need to be reloaded. If your dynamite is stable — that is, if it hasn't started "sweating" nitroglycerine — a sudden impact simply will not set it off. Case closed. The modern plastic charge is even more resistant to surprise explosions, so relax and save your bullets, friend. You might as well be shooting at a jar of Vaseline.

The traditional *flame* fuse is unpopular with modern criminals, since its relatively short burning time allows little time for escape, and the sputtering fuse itself provides audiovisual evidence of the bomb's location. Still, such fuses do crop up from time to time, on homemade pipe bombs and the like, sometimes with the addition of a simple timer.

Military and commercial fuses are designed with predetermined burning rates, so many feet per minute, so that time elapsed between ignition of the fuse and detonation of the charge may be controlled by trimming back the fuse to any length desired. Unless your characters are working on black powder bombs, the fuse itself won't detonate the charge. Instead, its business end will be inserted in a "blasting cap," a two- or three-inch tube of metal packed with sensitive explosive such as fulminate of mercury. This detonator will be wedged inside a primer charge, that charge inserted in the bulk of the explosives. When the crackling fuse sets off the blasting cap, a mighty chain reaction does the rest. (The primer charge is constant with explosives, whether it is detonated by a spark, a sudden impact, or electric current from a battery.)

A variation on the flame fuse was employed by Ku Klux Klansmen in the early 1960s, to assure themselves of ample time for an escape. Instead of using extra fuse with its attendant risks, the bombers trimmed it short and stuck the free end in a book of matches, rigging up a cigarette or candle as the timer. Once the matches were ignited, only seconds would remain before the blast. According to authorities, the Klan used such a bomb to wreck the 16th Street Baptist Church in Birmingham, Alabama, in September 1963, killing four teenage girls and blinding another for life. (In the two decades after World War II, racial bombings were so common in Alabama's industrial heartland that blacks nicknamed the city "Bombingham.")

An alternative method, the *chemical* fuse, normally uses a vial of acid, crushed inside some resistant container, providing lag time as the acid eats its way through to make contact with a chemical primer charge. (Britain's Angry Brigade used a combination of chemical and mechanical techniques, dripping acid on a retainer tape, which slowly burned through to release a simple striker.) Rubber condoms seem to be the average terrorist's favorite "timing device," but the technique is at best imprecise, the bomber forced to estimate how long a given dose of acid may require to eat through latex. Practice runs won't always do the trick, since purity and strength of acid may be difficult to gauge, and any microscopic holes or imperfections in a condom may result in a fatal case of premature detonation.

Most time bombs employ an *electric* fuse, with a clock or watch wired to link battery terminals when the hands reach a certain position on the clock's face, thus closing the circuit and sending a jolt to the primer charge. The Baader-Meinhof used egg timers on some of their bombs, and the IRA once purchased a batch of clockwork buzzers used to signal expiration on a parking meter. Both devices were entirely functional, but they were limited to a one-hour time delay, thus restricting their use to short-order bombings.

Moviegoers may be more familiar with another version of electric detonator, using spools of wire to link a plunger with the charge itself. Depression of the plunger generates electric current, which in turn sets off the primer in a system normally employed for heavy blasts on highways, mining operations, and construction sites. The plunger is entirely optional, as similar results may be obtained by hooking up the loose wires to a battery. Objections to this method are the wire itself, which may be subject to discovery and interference, plus the fact that bombers are required to maintain visual contact with their target, multiplying the risks of identification and capture.

The popular radio fuse — employing the same system used to control model cars, boats, and airplanes — provides greater security in the form of remote control. Armed with a strong enough signal device, a bomber may be able to detonate his charge from miles away, though some will still require a line-of-sight connection.

The Provisional IRA used a remote-control bomb to kill Lord Mountbatten in August 1979, planting their charge on his fishing boat at the family's home on Mullagmore Bay, near Sligo, in the Republic of Ireland. When Mountbatten set out one morning to check his lobster traps, the explosives were detonated by lookouts on a nearby cliff, killing the target and three other members of his family.

Israeli "Wrath of God" commandos made extensive use of remote-control bombs in their efforts to avenge the Munich Olympics massacre of 1972. In December of that year, agents lured PLO spokesman Mahmoud Hamshari out of his Paris apartment on the pretext of giving a media interview. In his absence, prowlers planted a bomb with a radio fuse in the base of Hamshari's telephone, killing him the next day when he answered a call and the phone blew up in his face. Six years later, in January 1979, Israeli hit men traced the architect of Munich's slaughter, one Hassan

Salameh, to his hideout in Beirut, making the tag with a remote-control car bomb. Similar devices are also popular with the American underworld, used to kill Arizona newsman Don Bolles and Cleveland mobster Danny Green, among others.

In their most basic form, *mechanical* fuses operate by pulling a safety pin, releasing a spring that may (a) cause a firing pin to strike the detonator, (b) close an electrical circuit, or (c) produce a lethal spark through simple friction. Commonly employed in hand grenades and letter bombs, mechanical fuses may also be activated by opening a drawer, turning a door knob, closing a window, lifting the hood on an automobile — in short, by any simple action that requires some object to be moved.

Variant forms of mechanical fuse include the pressure devices, detonating an explosive charge either through application of pressure (as in a land mine) or through its release (as in some "booby traps"). One such was used by the Irish Republican Army in October 1975, when bombers tried to kill Hugh Fraser, a Conservative member of parliament, at his London home. A neighbor, Professor Gordon Hamilton-Frazier, noticed the large parcel lying beneath Fraser's car and stooped down to investigate, resting one hand on the vehicle as he did so. The added weight was sufficient to produce detonation, killing the professor instantly.

Another interesting pressure device was outlined by Frederick Forsyth in his novel, *The Odessa File*. After wiring his bomb to the underside of a car, the would-be assassin connects vital wires to a pair of electrodes, separated by the width of a small light bulb. The delicate trigger device, protected by a condom, is inserted between the coils of the vehicle's suspension, allowing bumps in the road to compress the spring, crushing the light bulb and joining electrodes for instant detonation. Drawbacks of such a technique include the uncertainty of timing, and — as the killer found out to his sorrow — a vast range of difference in the stiffness of various springs.

A more sophisticated version of the pressure detonator is the barometric bomb, designed to blow on board an aircraft once the plane has reached a given altitude, with atmospheric pressure taking over. In August 1972, a pair of Palestinian terrorists in Rome seduced two English women on holiday, inviting them to visit Israel for a change of scene. The women agreed, and tickets were purchased to Lod Airport, in Tel Aviv. One of the Arab Romeos presented his paramour with the gift of a new — and loaded — tape recorder. At the last moment, both Palestinians backed out of the flight, pleading "urgent business," and promised to meet the women in Jerusalem. Unknown to the plotters, their tape recorder had been stowed in the luggage compartment, where standard El Al armor plating contained the force of its detonation during the flight.

Bombs Away

The average homemade bomb is basically a crude and indiscriminate device. Pipe bombs are a no-frills favorite of terrorist groups, from the Weathermen and Ku Klux Klan to Germany's Baader-Meinhof gang, with the latter group also using gas cylinders and army water bottles as bomb casings. In Northern Ireland, members of the IRA often use bundles of dynamite or gelignite with ordinary combustible fuse, relying on bolts, nails, and scrap iron to serve as shrapnel. In October 1981, the Provos used one such device, detonated by means of a wire strung along scaffolding, to ambush a bus filled with Irish Guardsmen en route to their barracks. While several of the intended targets were wounded, the only fatalities were two bystanders, including a widow and a Roman Catholic youth. (For what it's worth, it is traditional in cases such as this for spokesmen of the IRA to offer their apologies.)

Car bombs can be devastating in an urban center, with several hundred pounds of explosives set to blow during the rush hour, the vehicle itself reduced to flying shrapnel. In 1977, IRA bombers stole an entire fleet of bakery vans, priming some to explode and scatter loaves over Belfast while others were left locked and empty, thereby wasting hours of the bomb squad's time. Authorities in Northern Ireland have responded by establishing downtown "control zones," forbidding anyone to leave vehicles unattended, but yellow curbs are no protection if a kamikaze driver can be found, prepared to give up his life for the cause.

While some car bombs are designed to spread indiscriminate terror among civilians, the more common device is intended to kill a specific vehicle's driver or passengers. The simplest technique involves an electric fuse wired to the car's ignition, detonated at the turn of a key. (American practitioners have been using this technique at least since 1935, when a Kentucky prosecutor went up in smoke, and in the early 1960s, when Youngstown, Ohio, earned the nickname "Bombtown, USA.") When potential targets began checking their engines for "extras," some bombers shifted to using heat-sensitive plastic explosives, wrapped around the exhaust pipes to detonate as temperatures rise. Pressure devices — like the one that killed PFLP spokesman Mohammed Boudia in June 1973 — may also be used under car seats, nailing the unwary driver as he sits down.

The Irish National Liberation Army came up with a new wrinkle on car bombs in March 1979, in the assassination of Airy Neave, Prime Minister Margaret Thatcher's advisor on Northern Ireland. The bombers employed a double firing mechanism, with a delayed timer arming the bomb, and a "tilt" detonator — using liquid mercury — setting off the charge as Neave drove his car up a ramp, leaving the House of Commons underground parking garage. In October 1981, the Provisional IRA used a similar device to maim Major General Steuart Pringle, Commandant of the Royal Marines, as he entered his car in London.

Culvert bombs — dubbed the "Big Bang" by British security forces — are another favorite IRA weapon emulated by terrorists throughout Europe. An Ulster publication of the Bristish army, *Visor*, describes one such bomb for its readers.

> The device, dug into a roadside verge, consisted of homemade explosive packed into three beer kegs. Each keg, apart from containing fifty to eighty pounds of explosive, had a five to ten pound booster charge attached and all three kegs were linked to explode simultaneously. The mine was to have been electronically detonated and a command wire was discovered, partially buried along a hedgerow, which led to the firing point concealed in a nearby derelict building.

If undetected prior to detonation, culvert bombs are capable of turning autos, trucks, and buses into so much twisted scrap iron, overturning heavy armored personnel carriers in extreme cases. In July 1976, the British ambassador to Dublin, Christopher Ewart-Biggs, was killed by a 100-pound culvert bomb planted near his home, detonated by means of a cable traced to a wooded hill 300 yards distant.

In December 1973, Basque ETA terrorists began stalking the

prime minister of Spain, Admiral Luis Carrero Blanco, noting that he followed the same road each morning to reach his office. Renting a basement flat along Blanco's route, the killers tunneled twenty feet under the pavement, planting three forty-pound charges timed to blow one-tenth of a second apart, matching the normal pace of the admiral's car. A spotter kept in touch with the trigger man by radio, and on his signal the charges were detonated on cue, hurling Blanco's car over the roof of a nearby church.

On June 29, 1979, members of the Red Army Faction scored a near-miss on General Alexander Haig, then supreme commander of NATO, while he was driving to SHAPE headquarters in Belgium. More than 100 pounds of explosives had been packed in a culvert, radio-detonated by spotters on a nearby bridge, but their timing was off by some three seconds, damaging Haig's vehicle but leaving their target unscathed.

Letter bombs are less certain of scoring a kill, but they still remain popular with terrorists from Belfast to Beirut. Author Richard Clutterbuck describes a typical letter bomb, in *Living with Terrorism* (Arlington House, 1976).

> It is likely to be at least a quarter, and more probably, half an inch thick—so it will feel like a paper-back book or perhaps a folded report or pamphlet, rather than a simple letter. It will, however, probably feel heavier than if it contained the same thickness of paper. The explosive may "sweat," causing greasy marks, and there may be a smell of marzipan. The package will also bend in a different way, either giving a suspicious feeling of rigidity or an equally suspicious feeling of lack of elasticity—in other words, it may have the "dead" feeling of putty or clay, rather than the springy feeling of a pamphlet or a sheaf of papers.

Packed with three or four ounces of explosive, letter bombs generally fire by means of a "mouse trap" mechanism, cocked as the device enters an envelope, the striker released as the envelope is torn open. (An alternate method uses an incendiary fuse, producing sparks for ignition of the main charge.) On September 9, 1972, Dr. Ami Shachori, Israeli agricultural attaché in London, opened such a bomb in his office. Most of the blast was channeled downward, toward his desk, avoiding Shachori, but he was killed by flying shards of wood. Within the next few days, another fifty letter bombs were posted from Antwerp, addressed to Israelis and Zionists around the world. A second wave of bombs were mailed from Malaysia, days later, with a third batch posted out of India in November. One variant form, mailed from Karlsruhe, West Germany, was delivered to Dutch police by its suspicious recipient. Officers found forty grams of powdered cyanide in the envelope, primed to vaporize and produce lethal gas on exposure to air.

The Mossad began striking back in October 1972, firing off letter and parcel bombs to Palestinian resistance leaders in Algeria, Egypt, Lebanon, and Libya. Bassam Abu Sherif, a PFLP leader, was mutilated on opening a loaded box of "candy," with several other Arabs killed or wounded before the campaign ran its course. (Heavier parcel bombs—like the brightly wrapped Christmas packages mailed to certain Israelis in late 1972—contain larger explosive charges and are hence more likely to produce fatalities.) IRA commandos were so impressed with the Middle Eastern action that they launced their own campaign of letter bombs in August and September 1973, wounding thirty persons with an estimated forty bombs over six weeks time.

Booby Traps

My dictionary defines a booby trap as "a hidden bomb or mine so placed that it will be set off by any unsuspecting person through such means as moving an apparently harmless object." A secondary definition includes "any trap set for a person," and that's important to remember, since a number of the classics don't involve explosives. The first booby trap was probably Pandora's box, but Vietnam refined the game to something of an art form, with pits full of dung-dipped *pungi* stakes, snares designed to launch spring-loaded javelins from cover, vipers bound and dangling by their tails from the ceilings of countless VC caves.

So, who's the "booby"? *You* are, if you happen to be strolling through a combat zone in search of souvenirs, or wandering around a terrorist command post, hunting for the stash of secret documents that may include a list of members. In combat, there are endless opportunities for booby-trapping corpses, weapons, code books, canteens, a simple can of rations—anything, in fact, that someone from the other side is apt to handle with a minimum of care.

You needn't be a soldier or policeman to become the "booby" in a deadly game of tag. In 1905, Frank Steunenberg, ex-governor of Idaho, was killed by an explosive charge connected to his garden gate. Two generations later, members of the Synanon "drug rehabilitation program" tried to kill a hostile attorney by placing a rattlesnake inside his mail box. In between those disparate events, American headlines have recorded countless car bombs, letter bombs, electrocutions, and trap-gun incidents — including one case where a wounded burglar sued a homeowner for damages and won!

In short, if it exists, some artisan can make it lethal, using modern-day applied technology. The IRA is fond of wiring up abandoned houses, phoning in reports of some suspicious action on the premises, and sitting back to watch the soldiers or police set off a waiting booby trap. In August 1988, a man and wife were killed in Northern Ireland when they went next door to check up on a missing neighbor. Unknown to either of the hapless victims, members of the IRA had snatched their friend and primed his house to blow when the police arrived to check his disappearance.

Trip-wires are a common form of booby trap employed in buildings or in woodland settings, normally attached to one or more grenades. A sudden contact with the wire extracts the loosened safety pin, and by the time our target realizes what he's done, a close-range blast has cancelled all his worries. If your characters are short on hand grenades, the trip-wire method can be easily adapted to accommodate a dead-fall, hidden gun, or crossbow.

Pressure detonators, as discussed above, are often used for booby traps, in one form or another. Simple models may be used to booby-trap a chair or bed, a teeter-totter, an accordion — most anything, in fact, where weight or pressure is applied in normal use. The alternative pressure-release fuse is more useful in mining stationary objects, from telephone receivers to battlefield corpses, where shifting or raising the object triggers a blast.

Combustible or heat-sensitive charges have a wide range of uses for booby trapping. Depending on their size and the desired effect, they can be hidden in cigars or pipes, attached to stoves or ovens, carefully injected into incandescent light bulbs, drilled inside a piece of firewood, even sewn into the lining of a suit sent out for pressing. A variation on the theme involves combustibles that give off poison gas, as when the Minutemen, in 1964, considered slipping styrene plastic slivers into cigarettes for distribution to their enemies.

Tilt fuses are popular with booby trappers, and you don't need complicated mercury switches to nail your target. Doors, for instance, can be lethal. Your characters may tape a charge and battery against the far side of the door — that's away from the target — and about chest-high. The fuse consists of an empty test tube or plastic pill bottle, with two needles piercing the stopper and a steel ball bearing inside. Fasten same to the doorknob, with the needles uppermost, and connect the various wires to the needles. When the target — or anyone else — turns the knob, he automatically inverts the bottle and closes the circuit, blowing himself to smithereens in the process.

Hounded by security forces and bomb-disposal teams, professional terrorists have devised a number of antihandling devices, meant to detonate a charge if it's discovered prematurely. Some bombers use fuses sensitive to X-rays, thereby defeating attempts to study the mechanism from a distance. Photoelectric cells are also employed, primed to detonate on exposure to light — as when a car's trunk is opened or a flashlight is used in a dark basement. "Trembler" devices, activated once a bomb is set, use rolling metal balls or swinging pendulums to detonate the charge in case of any unexpected movement. In the modern world of terrorism, there are even secondary fuses, primed to blow if experts manage to disarm the primary fuse.

To Err Is Lethal

By the latter 1960s, homemade bombs had grown so numerous — and so apparently "simple" — that many prospective terrorists felt qualified to dabble in demolition without benefit of training or basic knowledge. Anyone can do it, right?

Well . . . not exactly.

The results of bungled bomb construction are inevitably startling, and many times they're fatal. Back in 1919, unidentified assailants tried to bomb the home of U.S. Attorney General Mitchell Palmer in Washington, D.C. I say "tried," because the bomb went off as they were placing it on Palmer's doorstep, blasting windows out of the adjacent homes. The bombers weren't identified, but two left hands discovered in the rubble told detectives that a pair of terrorists had gone to that great revolution in the sky. Fifty years later, in Maryland, a pair of black militants died while transporting explosives by car, and in March 1970 an explosion leveled the SDS bomb factory in Greenwich Village, killing three self-styled "freedom fighters."

Certain accidents may be attributed to use of obsolete commercial charges that have broken down and started "sweating" nitroglycerine, but most are caused by ignorance and common negligence. Some blasting recipes may lie inert until a primer charge is blown to set them off, but others are extremely volatile, igniting with a touch, or even through exposure to the air we breathe. Improper tools or careless handling of same may strike a spark and start a lethal chain reaction in the lab. Incredibly, some would-be bombers even smoke while working with explosives, and the FBI suspects that smoking may have caused the Greenwich Village blast in 1970.

Without a doubt, improper handling of electric fuses is the leading cause of accidental death for terrorists. The IRA experienced so many accidents with novice bombers that its expert craftsmen specially designed a safety pin, which has to be removed before the timer will begin its countdown. Next, some nervous types forgot to pull the pin, and so the Provos started marking them with tags, requiring bombers to return the pin and tag as proof of a completed mission. It appeared to be a foolproof system, up until the time one youth forgot the tag *and* label, thus providing officers with the address of his commander. (Nor is expertise a guarantee of safety. In 1974, the FALN's top bombmaker lost both hands and most of his face while planting a charge in Chicago.)

Radio fuses are another source of potential risk, susceptible to interference from the radios in taxis and police cars, even signals from remote-control TVs and automatic garage doors. In Northern Ireland, the advent of radio fuses prompted British troops to employ powerful transmitters, striving to detonate IRA bombs before they were planted. Several bombers were killed before the Provos got their act together, installing a new safety device to block premature detonation.

Grenades

First introduced in the fifteenth century, grenades waited 300 years to take their name from the Spanish *granada*, or "pomegranate."

Early grenades were spherical charges (hence the descriptive name) with combustible fuses, the latter prone to detonate prematurely or else burn so long that the enemy had ample time for a return pitch. With the demise of siege warfare, grenades fell out of favor, making their reappearance on both sides of the Russo-Japanese war in 1904. Proliferation in World War I and later years saw grenades evolve into distinct offensive and defensive types, using both explosive and chemical munitions. With a wide variety of models including high-explosive (HE), smoke, incendiary, and riot control, grenades are ideal for use by criminals and terrorists, as well as their opponents. Under existing federal law, grenades are classed as "destructive devices," and their possession is subject to various statute restrictions.

Grenades are generally fired by either time or impact fuses. Time fuses are the most common, based on simplicity, economy, and overall reliability. The typical time fuse employs a spring-loaded lever, held in place by a safety pin, and later by the thrower's hand. As a grenade is thrown, the lever flies away, permitting the striker to hit a percussion cap. This, in turn, ignites a "delay composition," with detonation of the main charge postponed for a period of seconds while the grenade is in flight. Impact fuses are more delicate and costly, striking a precarious balance between volatility in action and safety in transit. One common type has a small internal cavity, with a steel ball at one end and a fragile striker at the other. Initially restrained by a safety pin — and later by the force of acceleration in flight — the steel ball is thrown forward by sharp deceleration, impacting the striker to produce detonation.

High-explosive charges are destructive in themselves, but if you've ever watched a "human cannonball" routine, you know the blast itself may not produce fatalities. Some sort of shrapnel is required to ventilate the enemy, with early grenades relying on the break-up of a cast iron casing. Poor results were gained at first, with some grenades disintegrating into dust and others hurling three or four huge chunks of metal, so designers started etching grooves around the casing, inaugurating the famous "pineapple" design. Modern fragmentation grenades normally use a thin steel casing, with tight coils of notched, square-section wire inside, providing a more symmetrical kill zone.

A popular frag grenade among terrorists is the Soviet RGD-5, also manufactured by the Red Chinese. Light enough to be thrown over thirty-five to forty yards, the RGD-5 has an average casualty radius of eighteen to twenty-two yards. Chinese versions of this grenade were used against British troops by the Front for the Liberation of South Yemen, and the Viet Cong used them extensively in South Vietnam. The Carlos gang carried several during the 1975 OPEC raid, with one member—Hans-Joachim Klein—hurling an RGD-5 at police before a bullet ricocheted off his submachine gun and drilled through his stomach.

America's standard grenade of the Vietnam era, now considered obsolete, was the spherical M 26. Tipping the scales at one pound, the M 26 was alternately used for stopping North Vietnamese Army charges and "fragging" unpopular officers behind the lines, proving equally effective at both tasks. Stolen in bulk by the Baader-Meinhof gang in 1971, a shipment of these grenades was traced by the serial numbers to the Japanese Red Army and the Carlos syndicate in France. It should not be supposed, from the decree of obsolescence, that no specimens of this grenade remain available.

Replacing the M 26 as America's standard fragmentation grenade is the M 67, with an average throwing range of forty meters and a casualty radius of fifteen meters. For extra security the M 67's safety lever is retained by both the standard pin and a small wire clip, designed as a back-up in case the pin is accidentally removed. In practice, soldiers normally remove the clip first, leaving the pin in place until they are ready to lob the grenade at their target. A four- or five-second delay before detonation is standard on the M 67.

A variant of the M 67, logically designated as the M 68, is essentially the same grenade with a different fuse, incorporating a combination of the standard impact and time delay mechanisms. The M 68's impact fuse fires by means of an electric detonator and tiny thermal power supply, with action initiated by means of a percussion cap. The thermal power supply requires a second or two to generate sufficient electricity for detonation, but after that time has elapsed, the detonator will fire if the M 68 strikes a hard surface or is sharply jolted. As a back-up system, in case the impact detonator fails for any reason, the grenade's power train keeps burning on its own, blowing the charge by pyrotechnic action within a maximum of seven seconds.

Smoke grenades come in a variety of colors and sizes, with the standard U.S. model designated as the AN-M8. A burning type grenade, designed to generate white smoke for screening small unit activities, the AN-M8 is also used for ground-to-air signalling in combat situations, such as marking a helicopter landing field. The grenade's cylindrical case is constructed from thin sheet metal, containing HC smoke mixture and a chemical starter compound. Light enough to be thrown for about thirty yards, the AN-M8 generates smoke for an average period of 105 to 150 seconds.

Incendiary grenades are designed primarily for destruction of buildings and equipment, but they may also have grisly antipersonnel applications. America's standard incendiary grenade is the AN-M14, similar in appearance to the AN-M8 smoke grenade, but filled with a volatile mixture of Thermite TH3 and First Fire Mixture VII. In action, the AN-M14 generates a temperature of 2,200 degrees (Centigrade) for a period of thirty to forty-five seconds.

Riot control grenades normally generate the same gases — CN and CS — discussed in Chapter 8, but a number of innovative designs are available, including several from Accuracy Systems, in Phoenix. One such, the M452 "Stingball," has a one-second fuse designed to prevent throwback and achieve airbursts with a minimum of effort. The Stingball's casing is molded from soft rubber, with the explosive charge in a central pocket, surrounded by numerous marble-sized soft-rubber balls. On detonation, these are fired in all directions, pelting members of a crowd with stinging force and (hopefully) dispersing their formation. For a little something extra, Accuracy System's M45C, the "Comboball," includes a dose of CS gas to keep things interesting.

Stun grenades are another popular item with antiterrorist units, designed to blind and deafen gunmen, sometimes knocking them unconscious, with a minimum of risk to hostages. Accuracy Systems offers a full range of antiterrorist munitions, including the M429 ("Thunderflash"), the M470 Magnum, the M450 ("Multiflash"), and the M451 ("Multi-Starflash") grenades. The basic model M429 is specially formulated from cardboard, to minimize flying shrapnel, designed to produce a stunning blast and brilliant flash of light. The M470 Magnum provides roughly twice the

M429's concussive force, for use outdoors, while the M450 ejects seven distinct submunitions, emitting a series of blasts in a two-second time span. Finally, the M451 throws in the kitchen sink, with multiple blasts, dazzling flashes, and sizzling-hot sparks to stun and disorient human targets.

The Rocket's Red Glare

Terrorists are generally deprived of artillery, but in recent years they've made up the difference by resorting to use of portable (and often disposable) rocket launchers. Less than five feet long in many cases, modern air-to-ground and antiarmor weapons are designed for maximum mobility in combat situations, providing individual foot soldiers with the ultimate in firepower short of tactical nuclear weapons. Weapons like the American "Stinger" and LAW rockets (Light Antitank Weapon) have found their way into terrorist hands already, with various groups vying hungrily for newer, more lethal hardware.

The Soviet RPG-7 is standard equipment for terrorists around the world, provided by Eastern Bloc countries and makeshift production lines in the Middle East. The RPG's shoulder-fired launcher measures 39 inches overall, with a bore diameter of 1.5 inches, and weighs 15.4 pounds. The cumbersome rocket weighs 4.95 pounds and protrudes from the muzzle, sporting a payload 3.3 inches in diameter. Maximum range for a stationary target is 555 yards, with accuracy reduced to 330 yards for moving targets. On impact, the rocket can penetrate 12.6 inches of armor plating.

Widely used against Americans in Vietnam, the RPG has also surfaced in South Africa, in the hands of the terrorist African National Congress. Members of the IRA appreciate the weapon, and by October 1981 they had fired at least 185 Soviet rockets at British army posts and vehicles, losing twenty-one launchers in various raids. In January 1973, the Carlos gang staged two attacks with RPGs at Orly airport, trying to destroy El Al airliners, but the gunners missed their targets each time, damaging a Yugoslavian plane and an airport terminal building. On September 15, 1981, the Baader-Meinhof gang fired an RPG rocket at a vehicle occupied by General Frederick Kreusen, U.S. Army Commander in Europe, but Kreusen was spared major injury despite a direct hit on his armored Mercedes.

The Soviet SAM 7 "Strela" is a surface-to-air missile, measuring 51.2 inches overall, fired from a 53-inch portable launcher. Weighing 20.25 pounds, the rocket is powered by a three-stage solid propellant motor, with a maximum range of 3,792 yards and a maximum altitude of 6,560 feet. In flight, an infrared heat-seeking guidance system takes the SAM 7 to its target—presumably the engines of a fighter plane, military helicopter, or civilian airliner.

In the Yom Kippur War of October 1973, SAM 7s scored the few successful hits achieved by Arab antiaircraft batteries upon Israeli fighters. By that time, the weapon had already made its first appearance in terrorist hands, with the arrest of five Palestinians in Ostia, Italy. Renting a top-floor apartment three miles from Rome's airport, the guerrillas had two missiles in their closet when police arrived, aborting their plan to shoot down the first available El Al liner. SAM 7s were also used by the Zimbabwe African People's Union, downing two Rhodesian Viscount airliners during the bitter guerrilla war that resulted in the foundation of modern Zimbabwe. More recently, in October 1988, a SAM 7 was confiscated from IRA gunners in Northern Ireland.

The American M47 Dragon is an antitank weapon, tube-launched, wire-guided, and optically tracked by one gunner. In practice, the disposable Fiberglas launcher is supported on a folding stand, with the operator seated on the ground, the muzzle of the launcher resting on his shoulder. The rocket's nose contains a shaped charge and fuse, the middle section sporting sixty side-thrust rocket motors that operate in pairs. The gunner merely has to choose his target, keeping it in sight until he scores a hit, at which time he removes the tracking mechanism and attaches it to a new launching tube.

No Nukes Is Good Nukes

Since 1949, when wily Russians "stole" the so-called secret of the A-bomb, Earth has trembled on the brink of Armageddon. Rivalry between the East and West for ultimate supremacy and "overkill" for years obscured another danger, namely, that an individual possessed of raw intelligence and certain basic tools could build his own nuclear weapons, based upon designs long since declassified and reproduced in countless publications. In the age of Star Wars, S.A.L.T., and ABMs, a madman with a suitcase or a steamer trunk could hold the world for ransom.

Nuclear extortion isn't new in fiction. Ian Fleming set the stage with *Thunderball* in 1961, and countless imitators have pursued the theme in print, on television, and across the silver screen. One "original" author tried to set himself up for life, with an action series based on the premise of his villain stealing 100 nuclear warheads, one of same to be recovered by the hero in each of a hundred books! As you might suspect, the notion got stale in a hurry: the "great conspiracy" was dumped after three episodes, the author got canned after ten, and the series expired with unlucky thirteen.

America's first real-life nuclear threat was logged in 1974, when the FBI received a telephone offer to spare Boston in return for $200,000 ransom. It turned out to be a hoax, but news of the event soon produced similar calls from Los Angeles, San Francisco, and Spokane, Washington. In 1975, the Bureau received a one-eighth scale drawing of a homemade nuclear device, mailed by someone who allegedly possessed enough plutonium and high explosives to blitz New York City. This time, a dummy ransom packet was prepared, but no one ever came to pick it up.

By this time, Uncle Sam had heard enough. The answer lay in creation of a Nuclear Emergency Search Team (NEST), boasting a budget of $50 million by 1981, designed to ferret out potential "pocket" nukes and see them safely neutralized. Despite sophisticated training and the store of cash on hand, the NEST team didn't fare so well its first time up at bat. In Wilmington, North Carolina, a disgruntled employee of General Electric made off with 150 pounds of lowly enriched uranium, removed from a GE fuel processing plant, demanding $100,000 in return for his promise to keep the theft technique secret. NEST swung into action on command, but agents of the FBI had bagged their man before the nuke hunters managed to track down his radioactive stash, hidden in a nearby field.

We've come a long way from the invention of gunpowder and Li Ch'uan's timely warning against "tools of ill omen," but the basic nature of the game remains unchanged. We kill each other faster now, in larger numbers and from longer range, but I suspect the changes make no lasting difference to the dead. Thus far, no threat of nuclear extortion has been realized, but given human nature, I suggest we're talking "when," instead of "if." The day may come — and soon — when cities, states, and nations may be held for ransom by fanatics with a suitcase and a cause. The only thing we know, for certain, is that this time fiction writers got there first.

Appendix A: A Selective Chronology of Firearms Development

c. 1000 – Use of gunpowder documented in China
  1247 – First documented use of gunpowder in European warfare
  1411 – Matchlock firearms introduced in Austria
  1476 – Rifled barrels introduced in Italy
  1500 – First documented use of firearms sights, in Germany
c. 1517 – Wheel lock firearms introduced
c. 1525 – Snaphaunce firearms introduced
  1690 – British forces adopt "Brown Bess" flintlock muskets
  1793 – Percussion lock firearms introduced in Scotland
  1835 – Samuel Colt patents first revolver in England
  1836 – Pinfire cartridge introduced
      " – Samuel Colt patents his revolver in the United States
  1847 – Nitroglycerine developed in Italy
  1848 – Christian Sharps patents the "drop block" breech-loading action
  1849 – Jennings repeating rifle developed
  1850 – Henry Deringer, Jr., creates the original "derringer"
  1851 – Alfred Nobel develops dynamite from nitroglycerine
  1854 – Volcanic repeating rifle developed from Jennings design
  1857 – First practical rimfire cartridge developed
  1859 – Christian Sharps patents four-barrel pepperbox pistol
  1860 – Spencer repeating rifle developed
      " – Henry repeating rifle developed from Jennings/Volcanic designs
  1861 – First successful centerfire cartridge patented in England
  1862 – Gatling gun developed
      " – Confederate forces introduce first practical machine gun
      " – Peabody falling block system patented
  1863 – Palmer carbine developed, with first bolt-locking system for metallic cartridges
      " – Remington rolling block system patented
  1865 – Modified Gatling gun adopted by U.S. Army
      " – Remington begins manufacture of double-barreled "derringer"
  1868 – Peter Mauser patents his first bolt-action rifle
  1873 – Colt "Peacemaker" introduced (.45 Long Colt cartridge)
      " – .44-40 Winchester cartridge introduced for rifles

    "   – .45 Government (.45-70) cartridge introduced
1874 – .38 Long Colt and .38 Short Colt cartridges introduced
1875 – Jacketed projectiles invented in Switzerland
1876 – .38 Smith & Wesson cartridge introduced
1878 – .44-40 Winchester cartridge introduced for handguns
1881 – Hotchkiss 1.5-inch revolving cannon introduced
1882 – .32-20 Winchester cartridge introduced
1884 – Smokeless gunpowder developed in France
    "   – Hiram Maxim patents first recoil-operated machine gun
1887 – Britain adopts the first Maxim machine gun for military use
1888 – .303 British cartridge introduced
    "   – 8x57 (7.92mm) Mauser cartridge introduced
1889 – 7.65mm Argentine/Belgian Mauser cartridge introduced
1890 – United States adopts the Krag-Jorgensen rifle
1891 – 7.62mm Russian cartridge introduced
1892 – .30-40 Krag cartridge introduced
    "   – 7x57 (7mm) Mauser cartridge introduced
1895 – .30-30 Winchester cartridge introduced
    "   – United States adopts Colt-Browning machine guns
1896 – .32 Smith & Wesson Long cartridge introduced
1900 – .30 caliber (7.65mm) Parabellum Luger cartridge introduced
    "   – .38 ACP cartridge introduced
    "   – 6.5mm Mannlicher cartridge introduced
    "   – 7x57R (7mm) rimmed Mauser cartridge introduced
    "   – 8x57 JR Mauser cartridge introduced
1900 – 1901–First military use of shotguns, in the Philippines
1902 – .38 Special cartridge introduced
1904 – 8x56 (8mm) Mannlicher-Schoenauer cartridge introduced
1905 – .45 ACP cartridge introduced
    "   – 8x57 JRS Mauser cartridge introduced
1906 – .30-06 Springfield cartridge introduced
1907 – .44 Special cartridge introduced
1908 – .35 Remington cartridge introduced
    "   – German Army adopts first Luger pistol
1912 – .375 H & H Magnum cartridge introduced
1914 – .250-3000 Savage cartridge introduced

1915 – Anthony Fokker synchronizes machine guns with aircraft propellers
 " – First military use of poison gas, by Germany
 " – Production of first Beretta automatic pistol
1916 – Tanks introduced, by British forces
1918 – German Army introduces first submachine gun used in combat
1920 – .45 Auto Rim cartridge introduced
 " – .300 H & H Magnum cartridge introduced
1925 – .270 Winchester cartridge introduced
 " – First known use of Thompson submachine gun by U.S. gangsters
1930 – .22 Hornet cartridge introduced
1934 – U.S. National Firearms Act limits ownership of "gangster weapons"
1935 – .357 Magnum cartridge introduced
 " – .220 Swift cartridge introduced
1938 – German Army adopts Walther P38 to replace Luger side arms
1940 – .30 caliber US M1 carbine introduced
1943 – German troops employ first modern assault rifle
1945 – .257 Weatherby Magnum cartridge introduced
 " – .270 Weatherby Magnum cartridge introduced
 " – 7mm Weatherby Magnum cartridge introduced
1946 – .300 Weatherby Magnum cartridge introduced
1950 – .222 Remington cartridge introduced
1952 – .308 Winchester (7.62mm) NATO cartridge introduced
 " – .378 Weatherby Magnum cartridge introduced
 " – 7 x 61 Sharpe & Hart cartridge introduced
1955 – .243 Winchester cartridge introduced
 " – .244 Remington cartridge introduced
1956 – .44 Magnum cartridge introduced
 " – .458 Winchester Magnum cartridge introduced
1957 – .280 Remington cartridge introduced
 " – Soviets adopt AK-47 assault rifle
1958 – .222 Remington Magnum cartridge introduced
1959 – .338 Winchester Magnum cartridge introduced
 " – .358 Norma Magnum cartridge introduced
1960 – .223 Remington cartridge introduced

"   – .264 Winchester Magnum cartridge introduced
"   – .308 Norma Magnum cartridge introduced
"   – .460 Weatherby Magnum cartridge introduced
1962 – .22 Remington Jet cartridge introduced
"   – 7mm Remington Magnum cartridge introduced
1963 – .221 Remington Fireball cartridge introduced
"   – .224 Weatherby Magnum cartridge introduced
"   – .300 Winchester Magnum cartridge introduced
"   – .340 Weatherby Magnum cartridge introduced
"   – 6mm Remington cartridge introduced
1964 – .41 Magnum cartridge introduced
"   – .444 Marlin cartridge introduced
1965 – .22-250 Remington cartridge introduced
"   – .225 Winchester cartridge introduced
"   – .240 Weatherby Magnum cartridge introduced
"   – .350 Remington Magnum cartridge introduced
1966 – 6.5mm Remington Magnum cartridge introduced
1968 – New U.S. laws forbid mail-order sales of firearms
1970 – .25-06 Remington cartridge introduced
1971 – .17 Remington Cartridge introduced
1987 – U.S. outlaws future production of machine guns for
      civilian sale

Appendix B: Comparative Handgun Ballistics Information

NOTE: Both bullets and powder charges are weighed in *grains*, with 437.5 grains = 1 ounce. Muzzle velocity—that is, the speed of bullet on leaving the barrel—is measured in feet per second, with air friction reducing velocity over distance. Muzzle energy—the kinetic energy, or force, carried by a projectile on leaving the barrel—is measured in foot-pounds, a unit of work or energy equal to the work done by a force of one pound when its point of application travels a distance of one foot in the direction of the force.

Caliber	Weight (grains)	Muzzle Velocity (ft. per sec.)	Muzzle Energy (ft.-lbs.)
.22 Rem. Jet	40	2100	390
.221 Rem. Fireball	50	2650	780
.25 auto	50	760	64
.32 S&W	88	680	90
.32 S&W Long	98	705	115
.32 Short Colt	80	745	100
.32 Long Colt	82	755	100
.32 auto	71	905	129
.357 Magnum	158	1235	535
9mm Luger	115	1155	341
.380 auto	95	955	190
.38 auto Colt	130	1040	310
.38 Super auto	115	1300	431
.38 S&W	146	685	150
.38 Special	158	755	200
.38 Short Colt	125	730	150
.41 Rem. Magnum	210	1300	788
.44 Rem. Magnum	240	1350	971
.44 S&W Special	246	755	310
.45 Colt	250	860	410
.45 auto	185	770	244

Appendix C: Comparative Trajectories of Rifle Cartridges

NOTE: While firearms are theoretically aimed along a direct line of sight (an imaginary line running through aligned sights to the target), bullets actually fly in a shallow curve or parabola (called the *trajectory*), thus rising above line of sight in the early stages of flight, and dropping below over longer distances. Correction is required for scoring on a target outside point-blank range.

Caliber	Comparative Rise (+) and Drop (−) in Inches						
	100 (yds)	150	200	250	300	400	500
.17 Rem.	+2.1	+2.5	+1.9	0.0	-3.4	-17.0	-44.3
.22 Hornet	+1.6	0.0	-4.5	-12.8	-26.4	-75.6	-163.4
.222 Rem.	+2.2	+1.9	0.0	-3.8	-10.0	-32.3	-73.8
.222 Rem. Mag.	+1.9	+1.6	0.0	-3.3	-8.5	-26.7	-59.5
.223 Rem.	+1.9	+1.6	0.0	-3.3	-8.5	-26.7	-59.6
.22-250 Rem.	+2.3	+2.6	+1.9	.0	-3.4	-15.9	-38.9
.243 Win.	+2.6	+2.9	+2.1	0.0	-3.6	-16.2	-37.9
6mm Rem.	+2.4	+2.7	+1.9	0.0	-3.3	-14.9	-35.0
.25-20 Win.	0.0	-8.2	-23.5	-47.0	-79.6	-175.9	-319.4
.250 Savage	+2.3	+2.0	0.0	-3.7	-9.5	-28.3	-59.5
.257 Roberts	+2.9	+2.4	0.0	-4.7	-12.0	-36.7	-79.2
.25-06 Rem.	+2.5	+2.9	+2.1	0.0	-3.6	-16.4	-39.1
6.5mm Rem. Mag.	+2.7	+3.0	+2.1	0.0	-3.5	-15.5	-35.3
.264 Win. Mag.	+1.8	+1.5	0.0	-2.9	-7.2	-20.8	-42.2
.270 Win.	+2.5	+2.8	+2.0	0.0	-3.4	-15.5	-36.4
7mm Mauser	+2.5	+2.0	0.0	-2.9	-7.2	-20.8	-42.2
7mm-08 Rem.	+2.1	+1.7	0.0	-3.2	-8.1	-23.5	-47.7
.280 Rem.	+1.8	+1.5	0.0	-2.9	-7.3	-21.1	-42.9
7mm Rem. Mag.	+1.7	+1.5	0.0	-2.8	-7.0	-20.5	-42.1
.30 carbine	0.0	-4.5	-13.5	-128.3	-49.9	-118.6	-228.2
.30 Rem.	+2.2	0.0	-5.3	-14.1	-27.2	-69.0	-136.9
.30-30 Win.	+1.8	0.0	-4.6	-12.5	-24.6	-65.3	-134.9
.300 Savage	+1.7	0.0	-4.2	-11.2	-21.9	-55.8	-112.0
.30-40 Krag	+1.4	0.0	-3.4	-8.9	-16.8	-40.9	-78.1
.308 Win.	+2.3	+1.9	0.0	-3.6	-9.1	-26.9	-55.7
.30-06	+1.8	+1.5	0.0	-3.0	-7.7	-23.0	-48.5
.300 H&H Mag.	+2.1	+1.7	0.0	-3.2	-8.0	-23.3	-47.4
.300 Win Mag.	+2.6	+2.9	+2.1	0.0	-3.5	-15.4	-35.5

.303 British	+1.5	0.0	-3.8	-10.2	-19.8	-50.5	-101.5
.32-20 Win.	0.0	-11.5	-32.3	-63.8	-106.3	-230.3	-413.3
.32 Win. Special	+1.9	0.0	-4.7	-12.7	-24.7	-63.2	-126.9
8mm Mauser	+1.8	0.0	-4.5	-12.4	-24.3	-63.8	-130.7
.35 Rem.	+2.0	0.0	-5.1	-14.1	-27.8	-74.0	-152.3
.350 Rem. Mag.	+2.6	+2.1	0.0	-4.0	-10.3	-30.5	-64.0
.375 H&H Mag.	+2.5	+2.1	0.0	-3.9	-10.0	-29.4	-60.7
.44-40 Win.	0.0	-11.8	-33.3	-65.5	-109.5	-237.4	-426.2
.44 Rem. Mag.	0.0	-5.9	-17.6	-36.3	-63.1	-145.4	-273.0
.444 Marlin	+2.1	0.0	-5.6	-15.9	-32.1	-87.8	-182.7
.45-70 Gov't.	0.0	-8.7	-24.6	-48.2	-80.3	-172.4	-305.9
.458 Win. Mag.	+2.2	0.0	-5.2	-13.6	-25.8	-63.2	-121.7
.460 Weatherby	+0.7	n/a	-3.3	n/a	-10.0	n/a	n/a

Semiautomatic Rifle

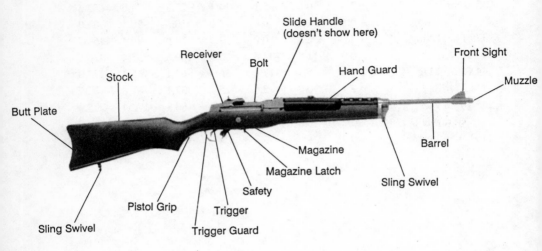

Slide Handle
(doesn't show here)

Receiver

Bolt

Hand Guard

Front Sight

Muzzle

Stock

Butt Plate

Barrel

Magazine

Magazine Latch

Sling Swivel

Safety

Pistol Grip

Trigger

Trigger Guard

Sling Swivel

Bolt-Action Rifle

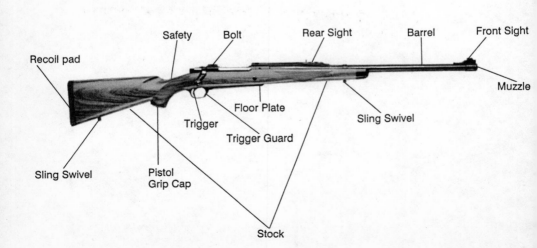

Safety

Bolt

Rear Sight

Barrel

Front Sight

Recoil pad

Muzzle

Floor Plate

Trigger

Sling Swivel

Trigger Guard

Sling Swivel

Pistol
Grip Cap

Stock

Single-Action Revolver

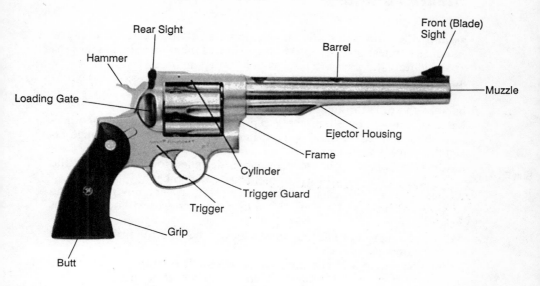

Double-Action Revolver

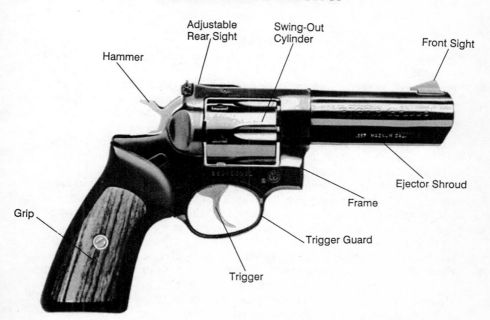

NOTE Items not visible on right-hand side of a double-action revolver include: 1. crane latch; 2. cylinder crane assembly; 3. ejector rod.

Firearms Glossary

assault rifle — any automatic or selective-fire rifle designed for military/police application (Despite recent misuse of the term in media reports, semiautomatic arms are *not* "assault" weapons.)

automatic weapons — self-loading firearms in which depression of the trigger results in continuous firing while ammunition lasts

barrel — the tube through which bullets are fired from a gun

baton rounds — "nonlethal" shotgun projectiles designed to stun or otherwise incapacitate rioters without penetration (though close-range fatalities have been reported)

bayonet — a knife or other sharp weapon designed for mounting on the barrel of a firearm, for use in hand-to-hand combat

birdshot — small pellets, in various sizes, used in shotguns for hunting birds and other small game, or for dispersing crowds without intent of serious injury

bolt — a sliding rod or bar that shoves a cartridge into the firing chamber as it closes the breech

bolt-action — a firearm equipped with a manually operated sliding bolt

bore — the interior of a firearm's barrel, from breech to muzzle (*see also* "gauge")

box magazine — any square or rectangular magazine, frequently spring-operated and detachable, designed for use with various small arms

brass catcher — a firearms attachment designed to catch and hold spent cartridges as they are ejected from automatic or semiautomatic weapons

breech — the rear part of a weapon's bore

buckshot — large pellets used in shotguns for hunting deer and larger game, or for antipersonnel applications

bullpup — a modern firearms design, in which a detachable magazine is inserted in the buttstock, behind the pistol grip and trigger mechanism

buttstock — the portion of a long gun braced against the shooter's shoulder during firing (also simply called the "stock")

cannon lock — the earliest and simplest guns, fired by applying a flame, live coal, or hot iron to an open touchhole at the rear of the barrel to ignite the powder charge

carbine — a short rifle, generally having a barrel shorter than 22 inches

cartridge — in modern terms, the cylindrical case that holds a complete charge of powder, along with the primer and bullet or shot, allowing a firearm to be loaded by simple insertion of the whole into chamber or magazine

centerfire — a cartridge with its primer in the center of the base

chamber — the receptacle for a cartridge (or powder and shot), from which the projectile is fired through the barrel

choke — constriction of a shotgun's muzzle, or the device used for achieving same, in an effort to regulate shot patterns

cock — *See* "hammer"

cyclic rate — the rate of fire for a given automatic weapon, measured in rounds fired per minute

cylinder — the rotating part of a revolver, containing the several chambers for cartridges

derringer — a short-barreled pocket pistol, generally single-shot or double-barreled, designed for maximum concealment

double-action — any revolver capable of firing its first and successive rounds by simply pulling the trigger, without manually cocking the hammer before each shot

drum — any round, spring-loaded magazine designed for use on various small arms

duckbill choke — an attachment for combat shotguns, designed to spread shot in a lateral pattern, along a line of advancing enemies

flash hider — a muzzle attachment designed to reduce the flash of fire produced when a weapon is fired, for maximum concealment at night

fléchette — a finned projectile of low mass and high velocity, used to increase the range and lethal penetration of combat shotgun rounds

flintlock — a modification of the snaphaunce, employing a hinged cover on the priming pan filled with powder, said cover being thrown back when the hammer falls, with the impact of flint on steel producing the sparks for ignition

full choke — the tightest available choke on modern shotguns, providing an average pattern density of 70 percent

gauge — a unit of measure of the internal diameter of a shotgun barrel, determined by the number of spherical lead bullets of equal diameter required to total one pound in weight; in Britain, "bore" is used as a synonym for gauge, as in "a twelve-bore shotgun"

general purpose machine gun — a hybrid automatic weapon, designed for alternate use with a bipod (as a light machine gun) or a tripod (as a medium machine gun)

grain — the smallest unit of weight in most systems, used to measure the weight of small arms projectiles and powder charges, with 480 grains equal to one ounce in the troy system of measurement

hammer — the moving part of a lock that by its fall or other action causes the weapon to fire (also called the "cock")

handguns — pistols

heavy machine gun — an automatic weapon chambered for cartridges of .50 caliber or larger, generally mounted on vehicles or in fortified positions

light machine gun — an automatic weapon weighing between 15 and 30 pounds, normally fitted with a buttstock and designed to be fired from shoulder support in a prone position, often with a folding bipod to support the barrel

lock — in any firearm, the mechanism that explodes the charge

long guns — any firearm meant to be fired from the shoulder, generally understood to include carbines, rifles, and shotguns

machine gun — a small arm operated by a mechanism, able to deliver a rapid and continuous fire as long as the trigger is pressed, generally chambered for use of a particular nation's standard rifle cartridge or (in the case of heavy machine guns) a specially designed load

machine pistol — a compact automatic or selective-fire weapon, designed for concealment and ideally capable of being fired with one hand

magazine — the component of a repeating firearm in which ammunition is stored, with a spring or other mechanism advancing fresh rounds to the chamber as needed (also called the "clip" in certain small arms)

matchlock — a primitive firearm, discharged by mechanical application of a hemp fuse, called a "slow match," to the priming charge

medium machine gun — an automatic weapon weighing between 25 and 60 pounds, normally mounted on a folding portable tripod

modified choke — on modern shotguns, a muzzle constriction delivering an average pattern density of 60 percent

muzzle — the mouth of a gun, from which the projectiles emerge on firing

muzzle brake — an attachment designed to reduce firearms' recoil by redirection of escaping gases

muzzle energy — the energy exerted by a projectile as it exits the muzzle, measured in foot-pounds

muzzle velocity — the speed of a projectile as it exits the muzzle, measured in feet per second

pattern density — the average percentage of pellets in a shotgun charge expected to strike within a 30-inch circle when fired from a range of 40 yards, used to measure the effectiveness of a shotgun's choke

percussion lock — an ignition system devised in the eighteenth century, in which the firearm's hammer strikes a sensitive chemical charge — fulminate of mercury in the earliest models — to detonate the priming charge in a secondary explosion

pistol — any short firearm designed to be held and fired with one hand; some authors refuse to recognize revolvers as pistols, but their logic — other than a fondness for semantic quibbling — remains unclear

revolver — a pistol designed with a revolving chambered cylinder that holds several charges or cartridges that may be fired in succession

rimfire — a cartridge having its primer in a rim circling the base

riot gun — a short shotgun intended primarily for use against disorderly crowds, sometimes employing nonlethal projectiles

safety — any mechanism or device intended to prevent the accidental discharge of a firearm

selective fire — a mechanism permitting alternation between automatic and semiautomatic fire on some weapons

self-loading — any weapon designed to eject one cartridge and chamber a new one, without manual intervention of the shooter, as each shot is fired

semiautomatic weapons — self-loading firearms in which one cartridge is fired and ejected, with a new round entering the chamber, for each separate pull of the trigger

shotgun — a smoothbore weapon designed to fire numerous small pellets, of various sizes, with each shot

silencer — *See* "suppressor"

single-action — any repeating handgun that requires the hammer to be manually cocked before each shot

small arms — firearms designed to be held in one or both hands while being fired; in modern terms, the designation includes pistols, rifles, shotguns, submachine guns, and machine guns (regardless of size)

snaphaunce — a forerunner of the flintlock, employing a hammer and flint to strike sparks against the weapon's priming charge

submachine gun — a lightweight automatic weapon designed to be fired with both hands, from the shoulder or hip, using standard pistol ammunition

suppressor — any baffled tube attached to the muzzle of a firearm, designed to minimize the sound of a gunshot

tubular magazine — a tube, normally mounted below the barrel in many shotguns and some repeating rifles, that contains reserve ammunition ready for firing

wheel lock — an early firearm discharged by spinning a serrated metal wheel against a flint to produce sparks, which flash through the touchhole to ignite a priming charge

Bibliography

Avery, Ralph. *Combat Loads for the Sniper Rifle.* Delta Press.

Bearse, Ray. *Sporting Arms of the World.* Harper & Row, 1976.

Bishop, Chris, and Ian Drury. *Combat Guns.* Chartwell Books, 1987.

Brown, M.L. *Firearms in Colonial America.* Smithsonian Institution Press, 1980.

Clede, Bill. *Police Handgun Manual.* Delta Press.

————. *Police Shotgun Manual.* Delta Press.

Davis, Tenney. *The Chemistry of Powder and Explosives.* Delta Press.

Dmitrieff, G. *Expedient Hand Grenades.* Delta Press.

Dobson, Christopher, and Ronald Payne. *The Terrorists: Their Weapons, Leaders and Tactics.* Facts on File, 1982.

Foss, Christopher. *Jane's Armour and Artillery.* Jane's Publishing (annual revised volumes).

Gambordella, Ted. *Weapons of the Street.* Paladin Press, 1984.

Garavaglia, Louis, and Charles Worman. *Firearms of the American West, 1803-1865.* University of New Mexico Press, 1983.

Hastings, Macdonald. *The Shotgun: A Social History.* David & Charles, 1981.

Helmer, William. *The Gun That Made the Twenties Roar.* Gun Room Press.

Hogg, Ian. *Jane's Infantry Weapons.* Jane's Publishing (annual volumes).

Lecker, Seymour. *Improvised Explosives.* Delta Press.

Lesce, Tony. *The Shotgun in Combat.* Delta Press.

Long, Duncan. *Assault Pistols, Rifles and Submachine Guns.* Delta Press.

————. *Modern Ballistic Armor.* Delta Press.

————. *Modern Sniper Rifles.* Delta Press.

————. *Streetsweepers.* [Combat Shotguns] Delta Press.

Markham, George. *Guns of the Elite.* Delta Press.

Owen, J.I., ed. *Brassey's Infantry Weapons of the World.* Pergamon Press, 1979.

————. *Infantry Weapons of the Armies of Africa, the Orient and Latin America.* Pergamon Press, 1980.

————. *Infantry Weapons of the NATO Armies.* Pergamon Press, 1980.

————. *Infantry Weapons of the Warsaw Pact Armies.* Pergamon Press, 1980.

Rapp, Burt. *The Police Sniper.* Delta Press.

Robinson, Roger. *The Police Shotgun Manual.* C.C. Thomas, 1973.

Shooter's Bible. Stoeger Publishing (annual volumes).

Skillen, Charles. *Combat Shotgun Training.* C.C. Thomas, 1982.

Smith, Joseph E. *Small Arms of the World.* Galahad Books.

Swearengen, Thomas. *World's Fighting Shotguns.* THB Enterprises, 1978.

Trzoniec, Stanley. *Handloader's Guide.* Stoeger, 1985.

Walter, John. *The Airgun Book.* Stackpole Books, 1981.

Wilber, Charles. *Ballistic Science for the Law Enforcement Officer.* C.C. Thomas, 1977.

————. *Forensic Biology for the Law Enforcement Officer.* C.C. Thomas, 1974.

Wilson, Nolan. *Firearms Silencers.* Delta Press.

————. *The Silencer Cookbook.* Delta Press.

Index